WE
POSSIBILITARIANS
ONE

ISBN-13: 978-1-959984-49-8

Library of Congress Number: requested

05-24-2024

WE ARE AT THE BEGINNING OF
THE POSSIBILITARIAN TAKEOVER OF
SOCIETY. WE HEREWITH DISPOSE OF
THE INCOMPETENT RULING CLASS BY
UNDERTHROWING IT FROM THE TOES
UP, & WE IMMEDIATELY IMPLEMENT
THE 1000 ALTERNATIVES TO THE
DESTRUCTIVE HABITS OF CAPITALISM.

POLITICS MUST ABANDON ITS
TRADITIONAL WAR & WEAPONS
PREOCCUPATIONS & MAKE THE
SEVERE HEALTH ISSUES OF OUR ONE
AND ONLY MOTHER EARTH AND HER
EARTHLINGS ITS PRIMARY CONCERN.

THE TERM "POSSIBILITARIAN"
APPROXIMATES THE WORD
"MÖGLICHKEITSMENSCH" IN ROBERT
MUSIL'S NOVEL, "THE MAN WITHOUT
QUALITIES", & HAS BEEN WIDELY USED IN
BREAD & PUPPET PRODUCTIONS.

WE POSSIBILITARIAN

+ NORTHEAST KINGDOM
+ PEACE + HARMONY TERRORISTS

MUST DEFEAT

THE FREEDOM + DEMOCRACY
MASSMURDERERS WITH THE
HELP OF OUR MAJORITY
UNDERNEATH THE MAJORITY

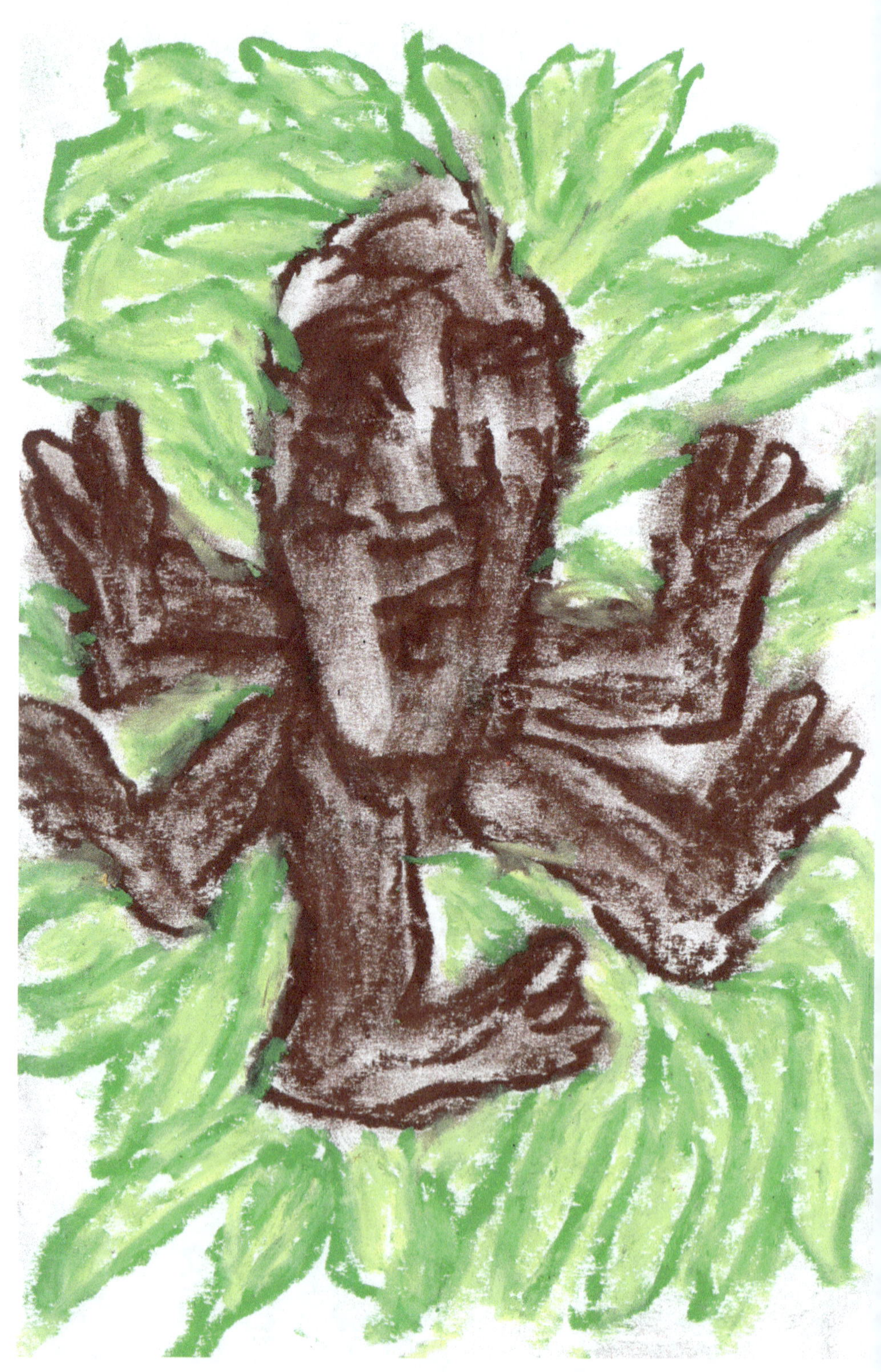

WE POSSIBILITARIAN
PEACE + HARMONY
TERRORISTS OF THE
NORTH EAST KINGDOM
REALIZE THE NEED
FOR PROPER FUNERAL-
IZATION SERVICES
FOR THE DYING
WESTERN CIVILIZATION
+ ITS FAKE MORALITY
HERE + EVERYWHERE
WHICH COLLAPSED

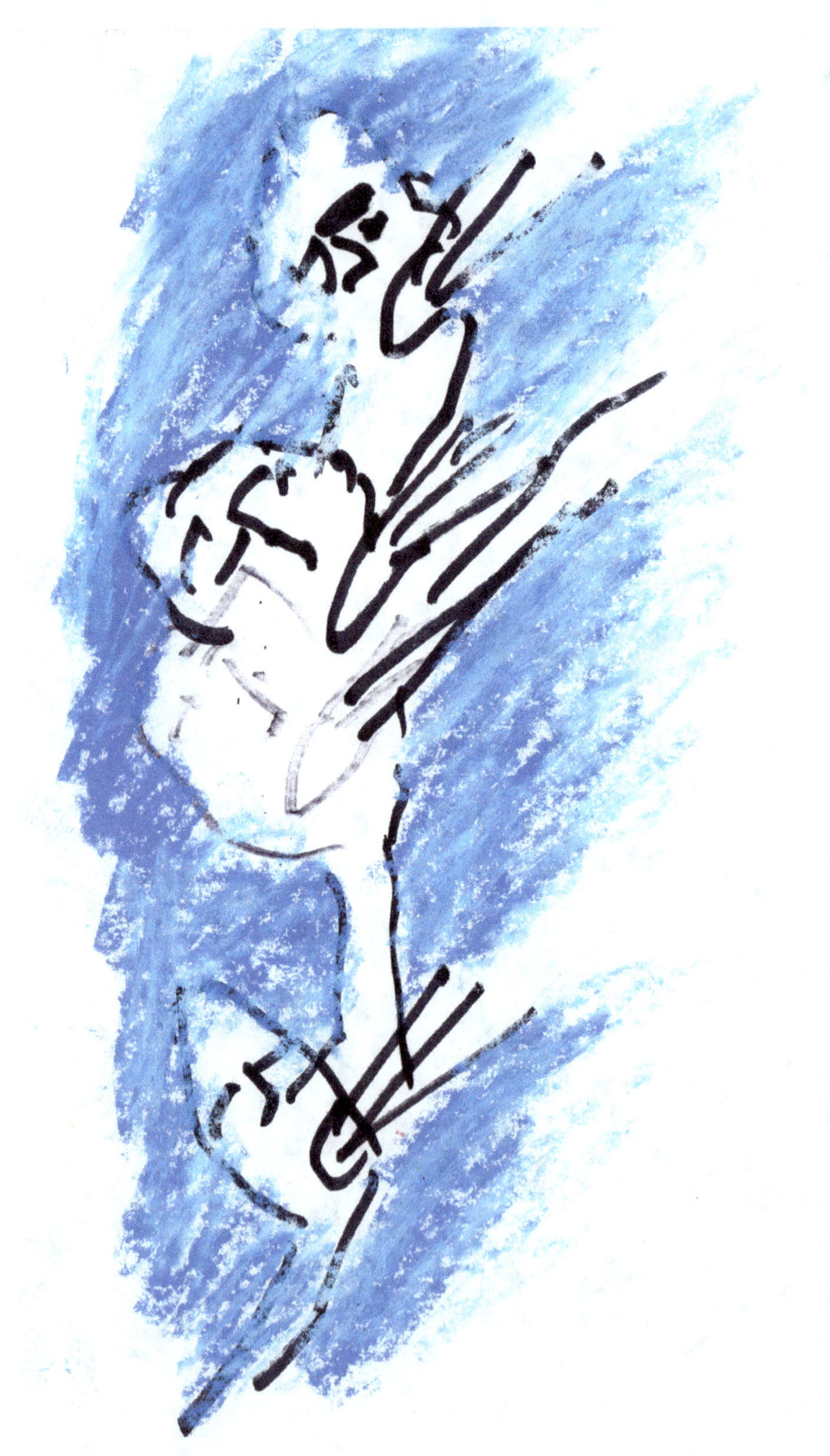

UNDER THE RUBBLE
OF US-ENGINEERED
ISRAELI BOMBARDMENTS
PERMANENTLY DISGUST-
ING TO ALL HUMAN
SENSE + DIGNITY +
INSPIRES THE DISINTEGRATION
OF THE FAKE IN ORDER
TO MAKE PLACE FOR THE
REAL: THE KROPOTKIN-
GUIDED MUTUAL AID
AS THE PRINCIPLE
MOTIVATION OF BEHAVIOR
+ AIMS FOR THE

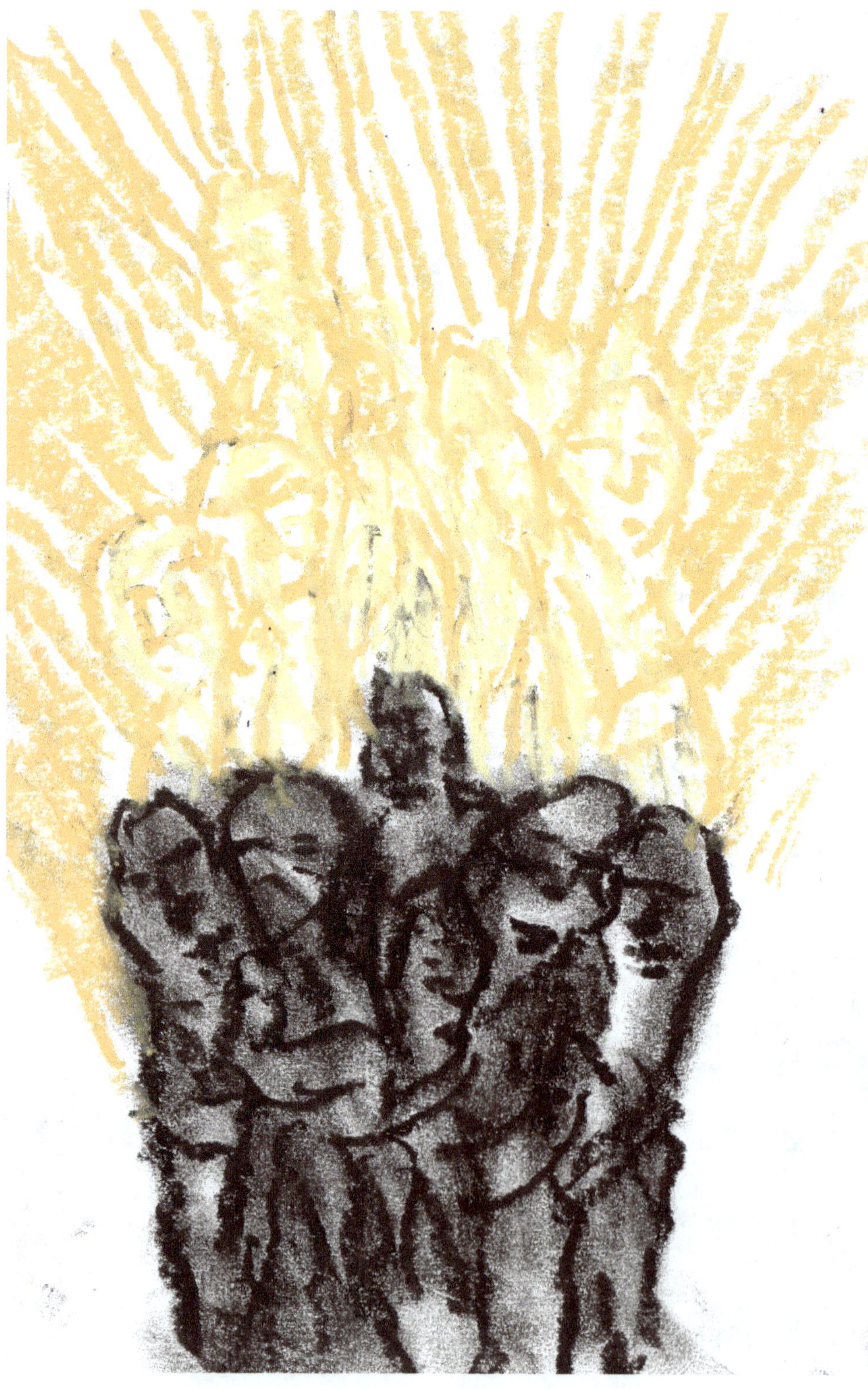

OBLIGATORY UTOPIA BASED ON E. BLOCH'S _PRINCIPLE OF HOPE_, THE HISTORY OF UTOPIA + THE POSSIBILITARIAN STEP-BY-STEP GUIDANCE TO OBLIGATORY UTOPIA. ONLY BY PURSUING THESE CONCRETE PROPOSALS OF ABANDONING THE FAKE PURSUIT OF CAPITALIST HAPPINESS CAN WE SAVE OUR SEVERELY DAMAGED SOULS FROM THE EMPIRE'S EXTERMINATION POLICIES AS PRACTICED RIGHT NOW IN PALESTINE. WE NEED MORE THAN: NOT IN OUR NAME NOT WITH OUR MONEY! WE NEED AGGRESSIVE ELEMENTARY

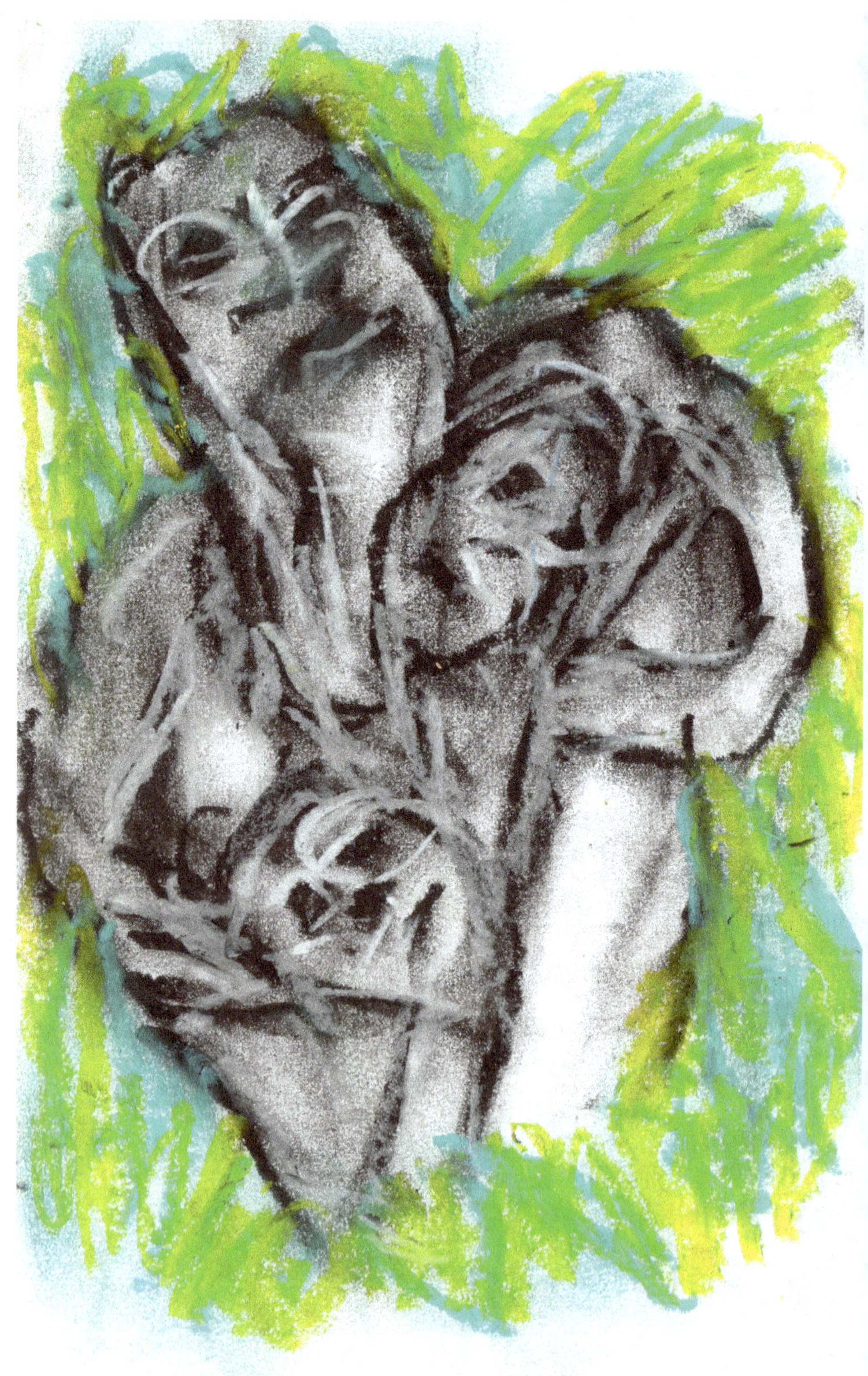

COMPREHENSION OF THE WHOLE, OPPOSITE THE ACCUMULATED EVIL OF THE WHOLE. THE WHOLE OF OUR BIRTHRIGHT'S EUPHORIA, OUR EVERY DAY PRACTICE OF OUR BIRTHRIGHT, OUR SURVIVAL KIT.

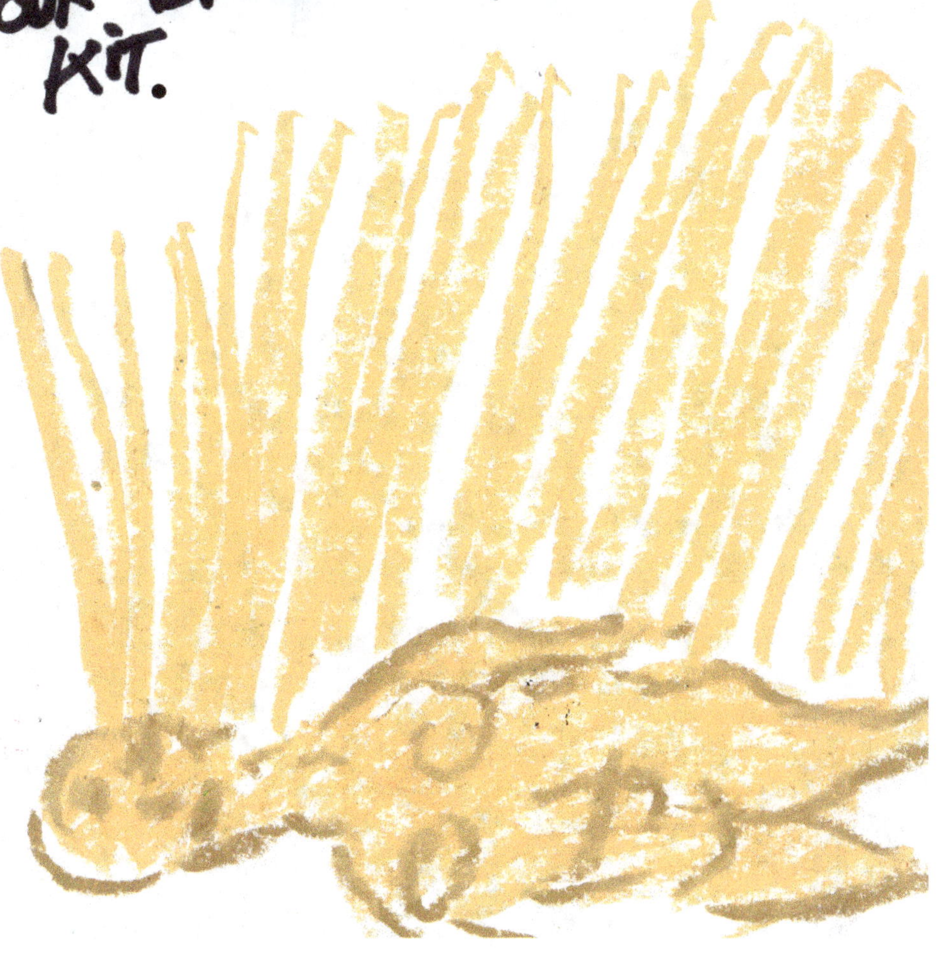

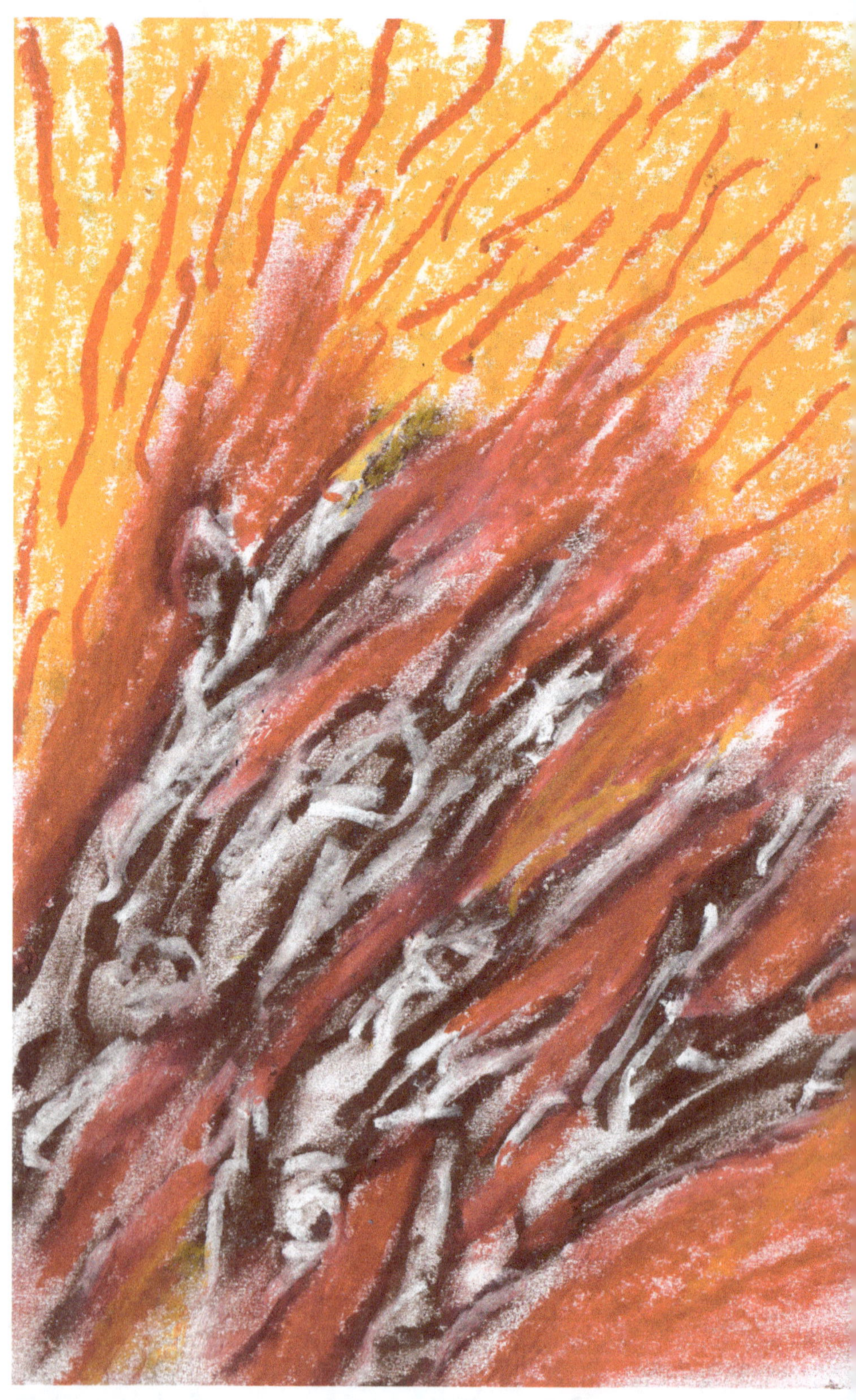

WE POSSIBILITARIANS

SHIT ON THE ARSEHOLES
WHO ASSIGN THE TERM
TERRORIST TO OPPONENTS
OF THEIR GENOCIDAL PURSUITS
WITH THE HELP OF THE TRUTH
INDUSTRY'S PROPAGANDA

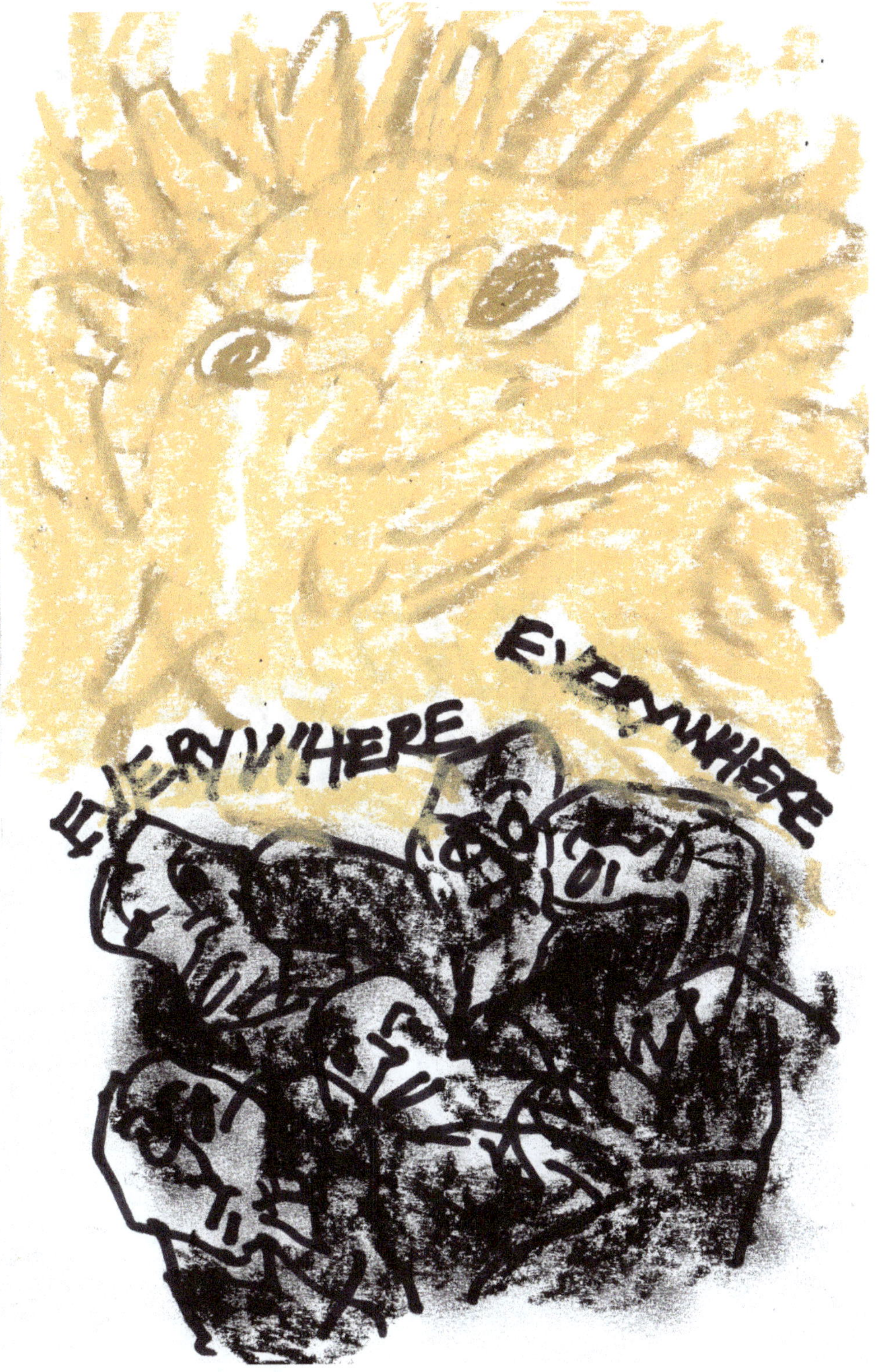

EVERYWHERE
EVERYWHERE

FUNERALIZATION SERVICES

MOTHER DIRT'S POTENT DIRT TO BURY HOMO SAPIENS, THE ARROGANT OFFICER IN CHARGE OF WESTERN CIVILIZATION'S DECLINE

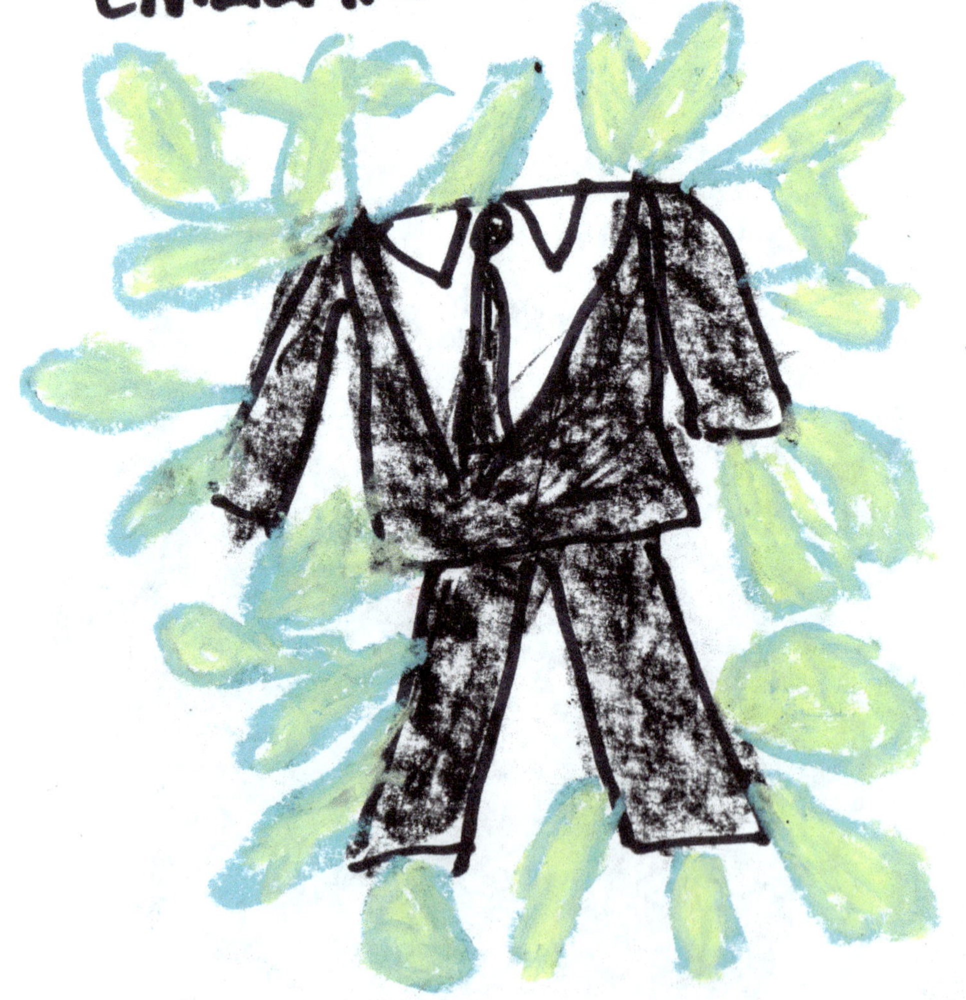

THE SCREAMING UNDERNEATH,
THE BOMBS AMPLIFIED TO
PENETRATE THE EARS OF THE
PILOTS + THEIR EVIL COMMANDERS,
TO DEMONSTRATE THE PILOTS'
DAMAGED MINDS WHO NEGLECTED
CONSULTING WITH THEIR OWN
MOTHERS + GRANDMAS + ARE NOW
CONDEMNED BY THE WORLD-
AT LARGE.

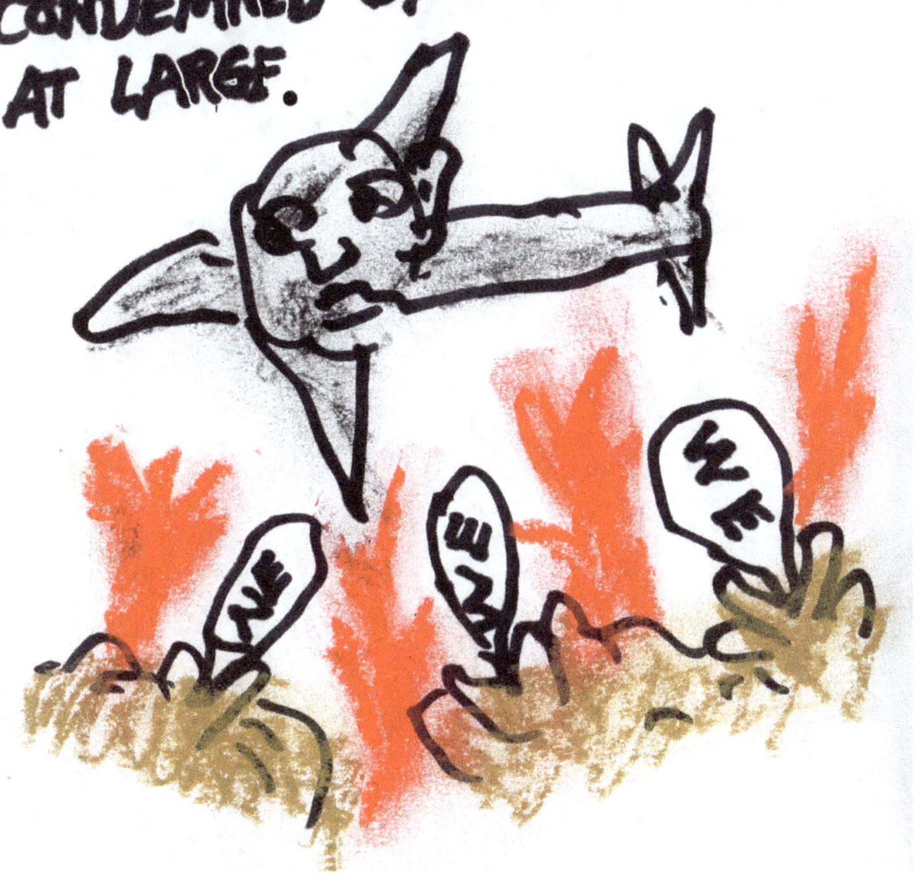

ALL PRIESTS OF ALL RELIGIONS
MUST SCREAM PALESTINIAN MOTHERS'
SCREAMS TILL HEARING IS
RESTORED IN THE EARS OF
THE FACILITATORS OF EVIL
TO AVOID THE HELLFIRE WHICH
is LICKING AT THEIR TOES

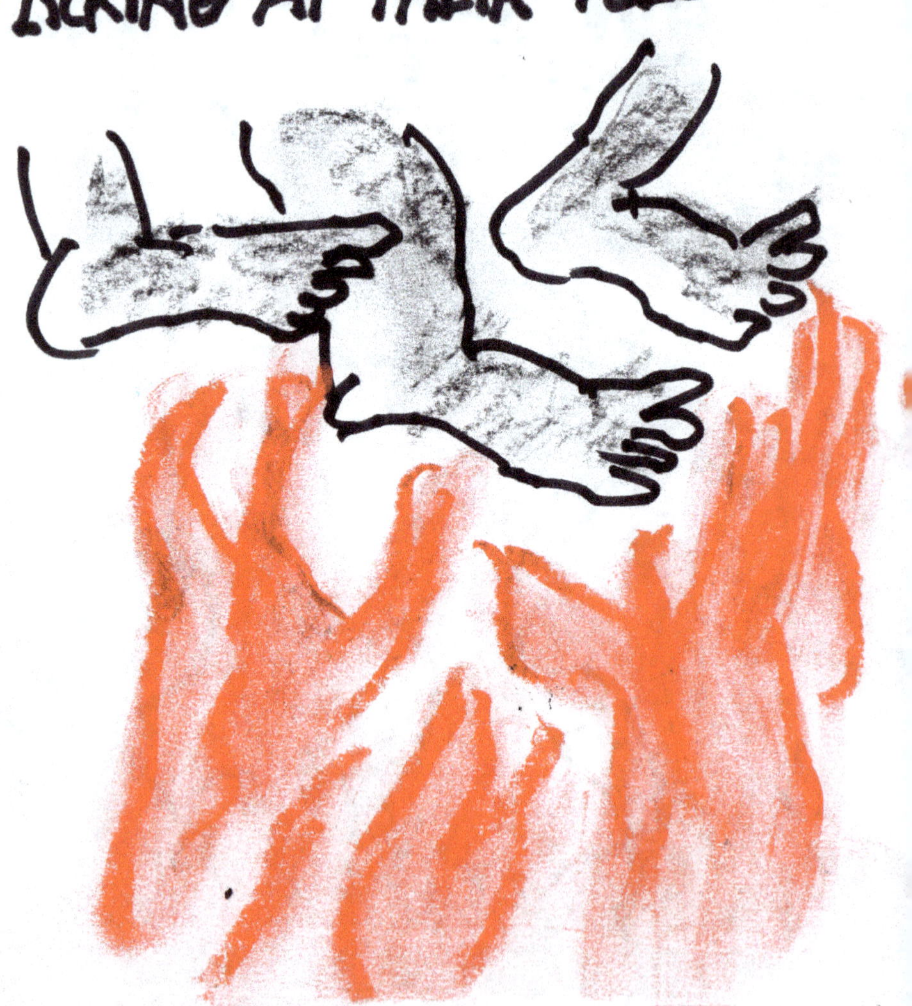

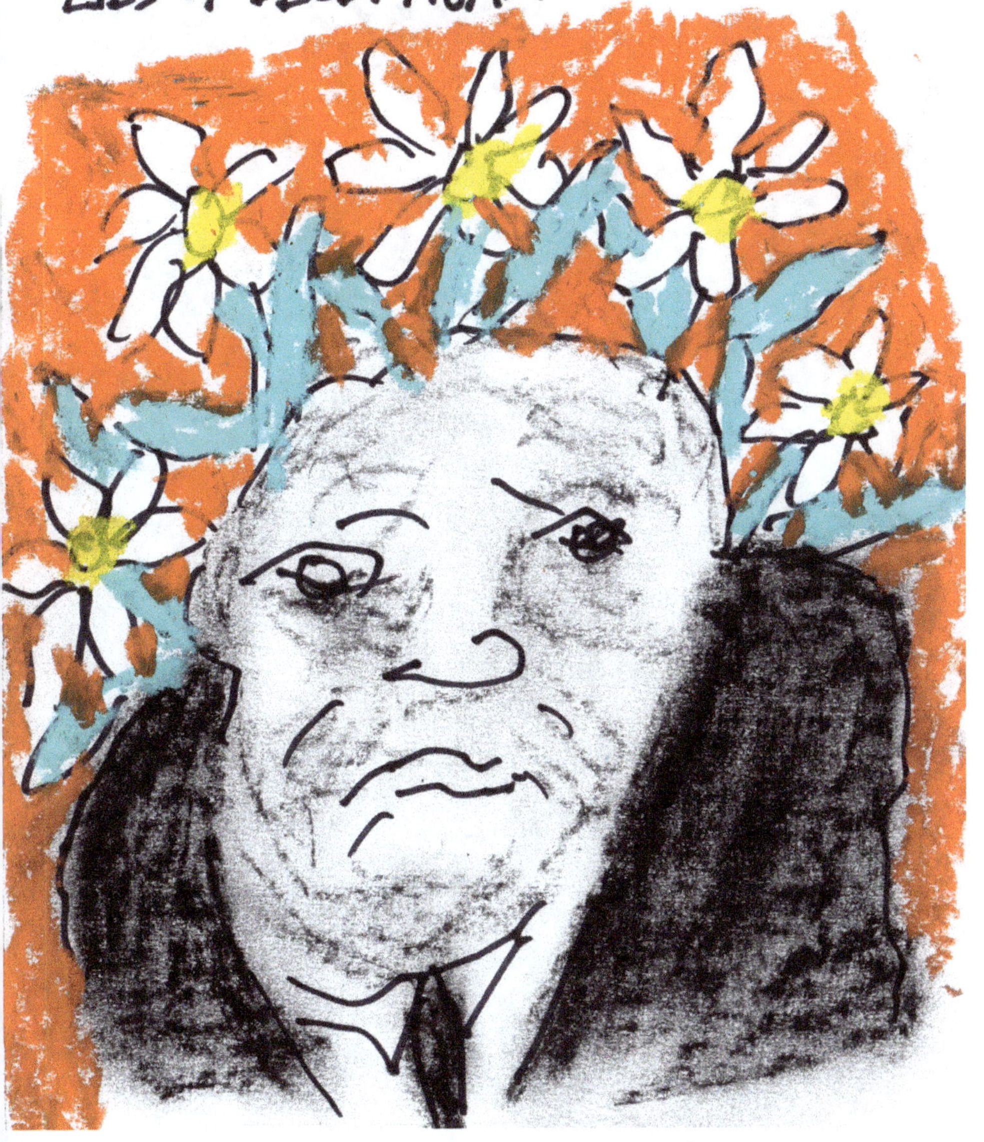

THE CORRUPTED BRAIN OF
ACADEMIA SPROUTS ORDINARY
EVERYDAY DAISIES TO CELEBRATE
LIBERATION FROM EMPIRE-INFLICTED
LIES + DECEPTIONS.

MONEY ITSELF, THE HABITUAL GOD OF ALL KILLER WEAPONS + THEIR CONSEQUENT PAINS IS NOW WIDELY RIDICULED + TRAMPLED UNDER THE FEET OF GARBAGE-DANCERS + ANTI-MONEY ACROBATS

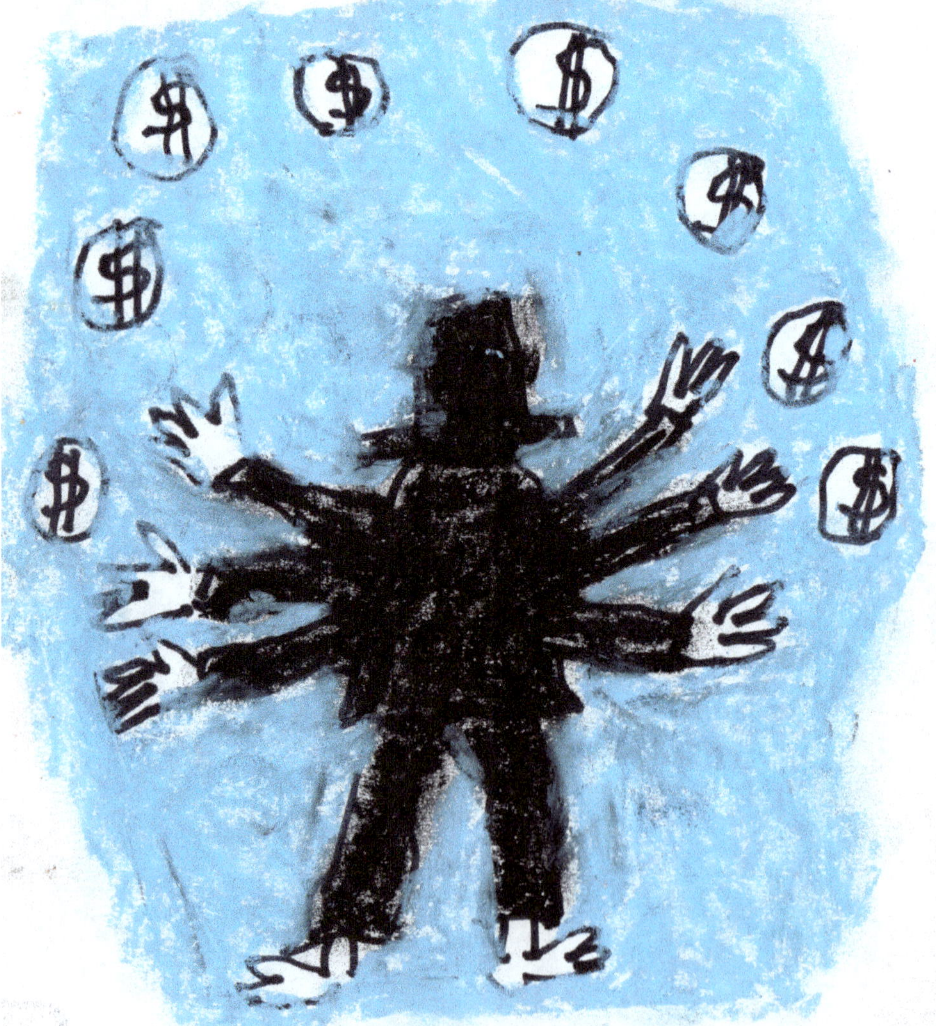

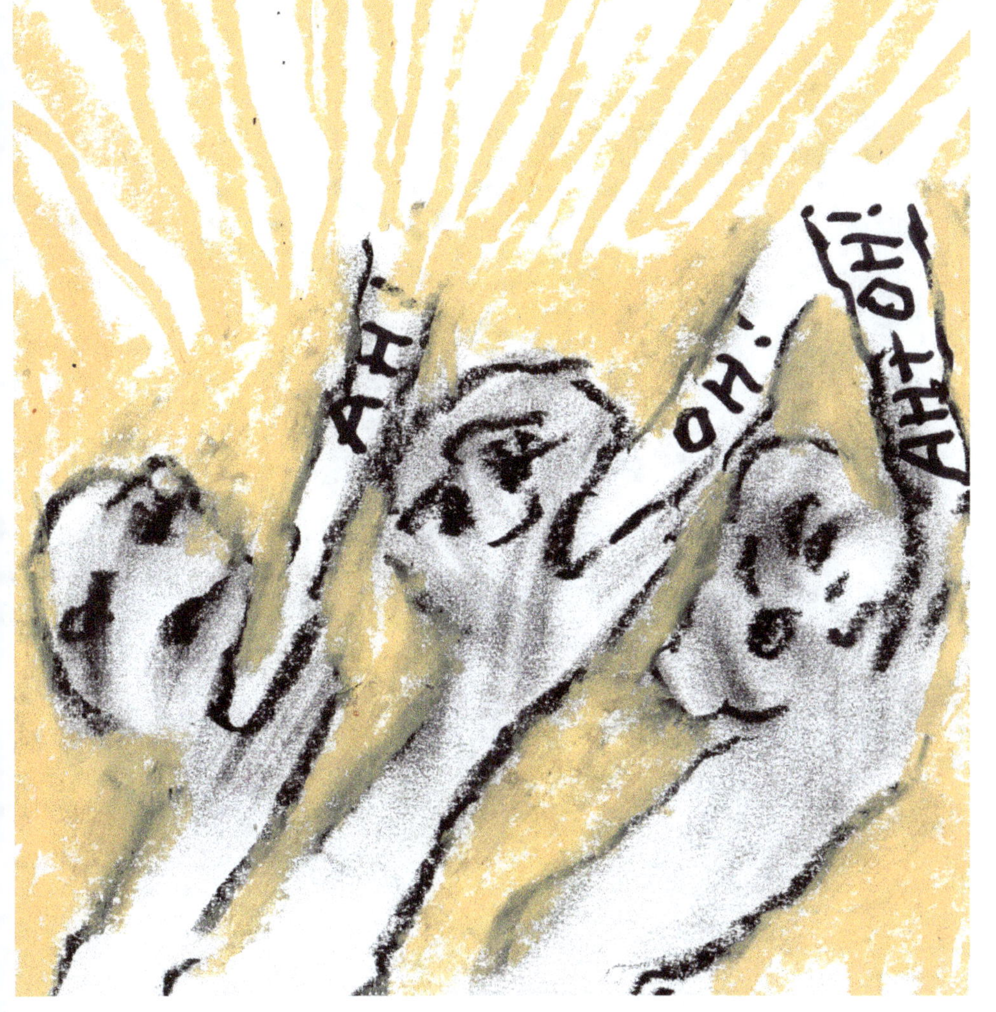

THE ORIGINAL AH!
+ OH! OF OUR HEART-OF-
THE-MATTER EXISTENCE
URGENTLY NEED NEW
VOCALIZATIONS+SYMPHONIES!

WE ARE NE K PEACE +
HARMONY TERRORISTS!
WE ARE POSSIBILITARIANS
WE MUST DEFEAT THESE
MASSMURDERERS

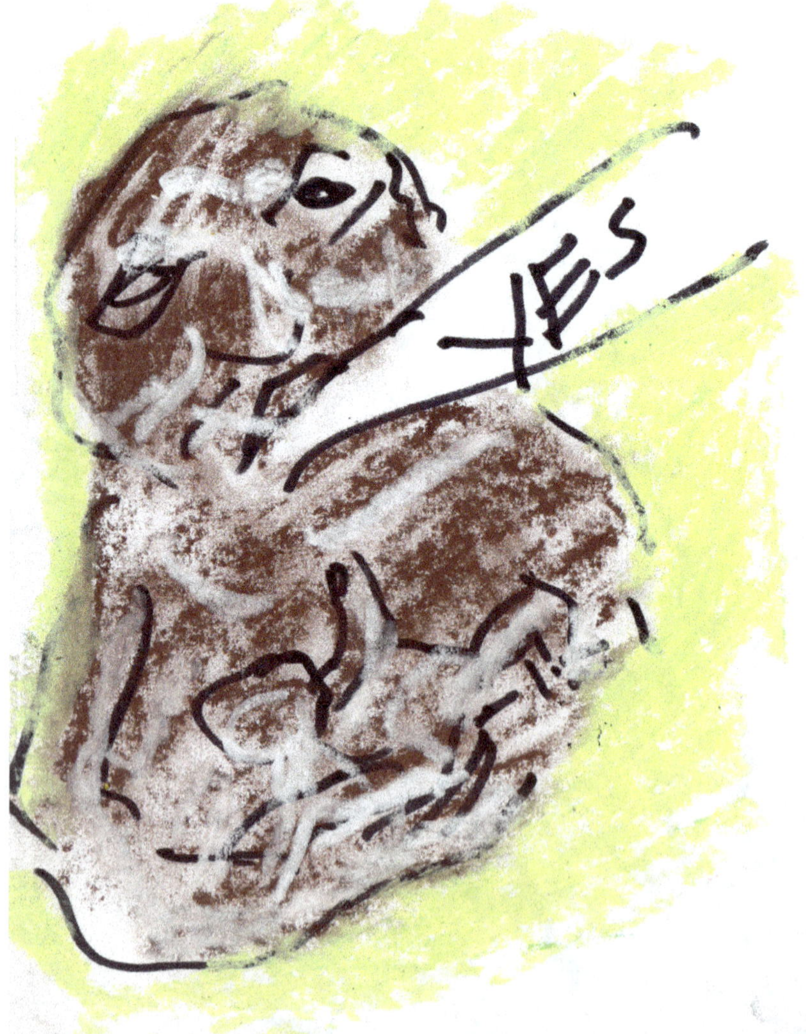

WE POSIBILITARIANS

DEFY RIDICULE

MAKE OBSOLETE

WESTERN CIVILIZATION'S

HYPOCRISY

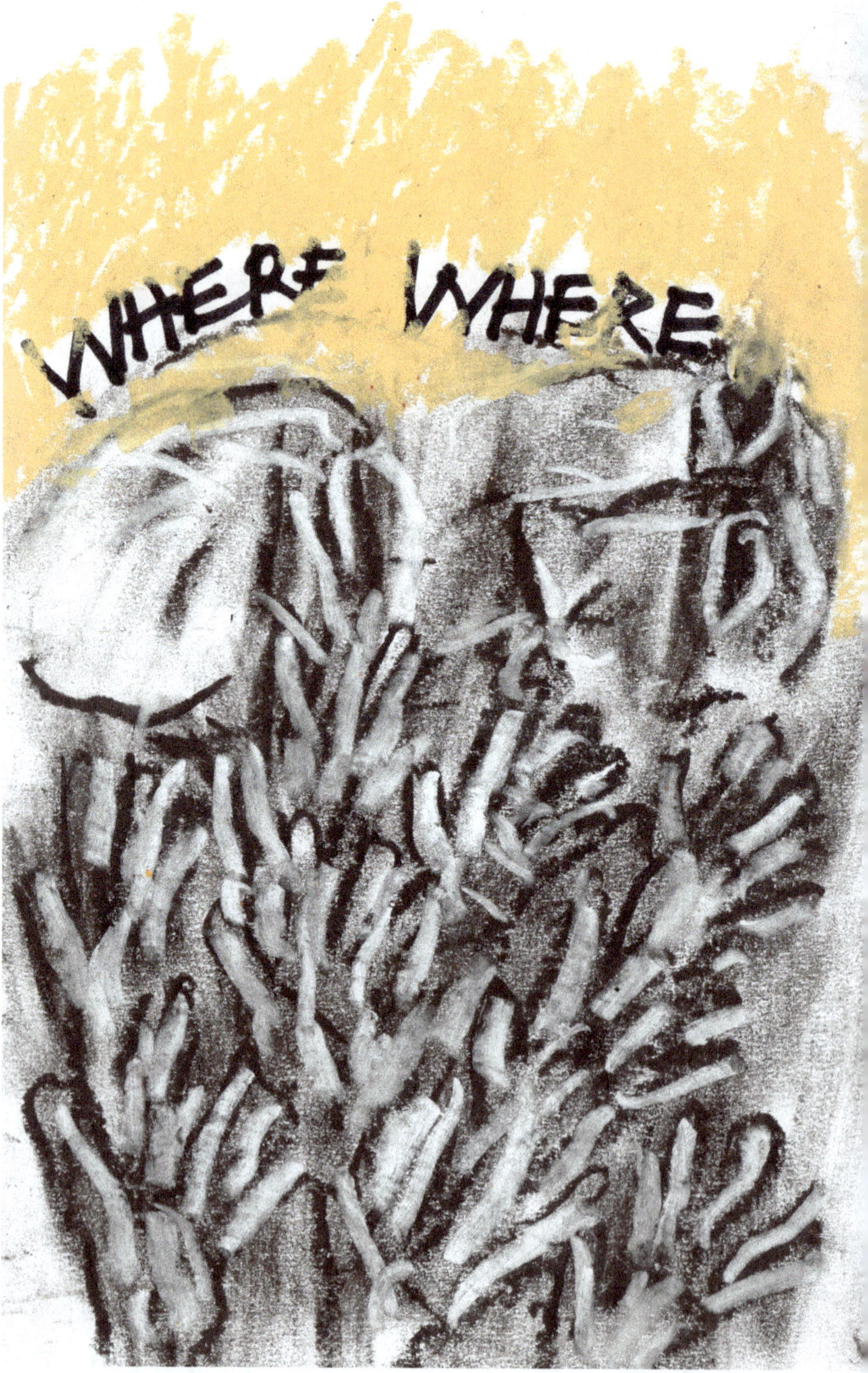

WHERE WHERE

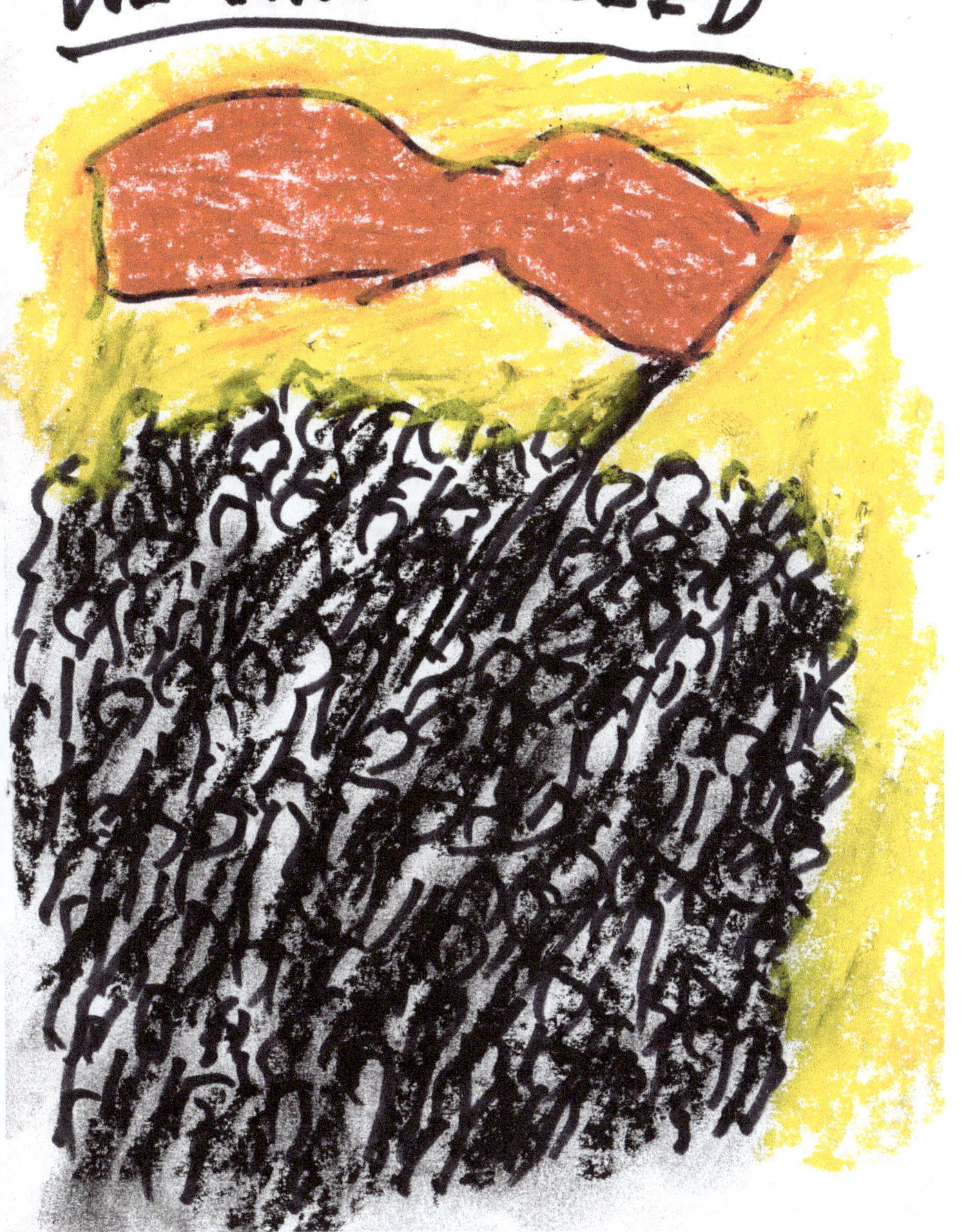
WE ARE NOT ALONE
WE WILL SUCCEED

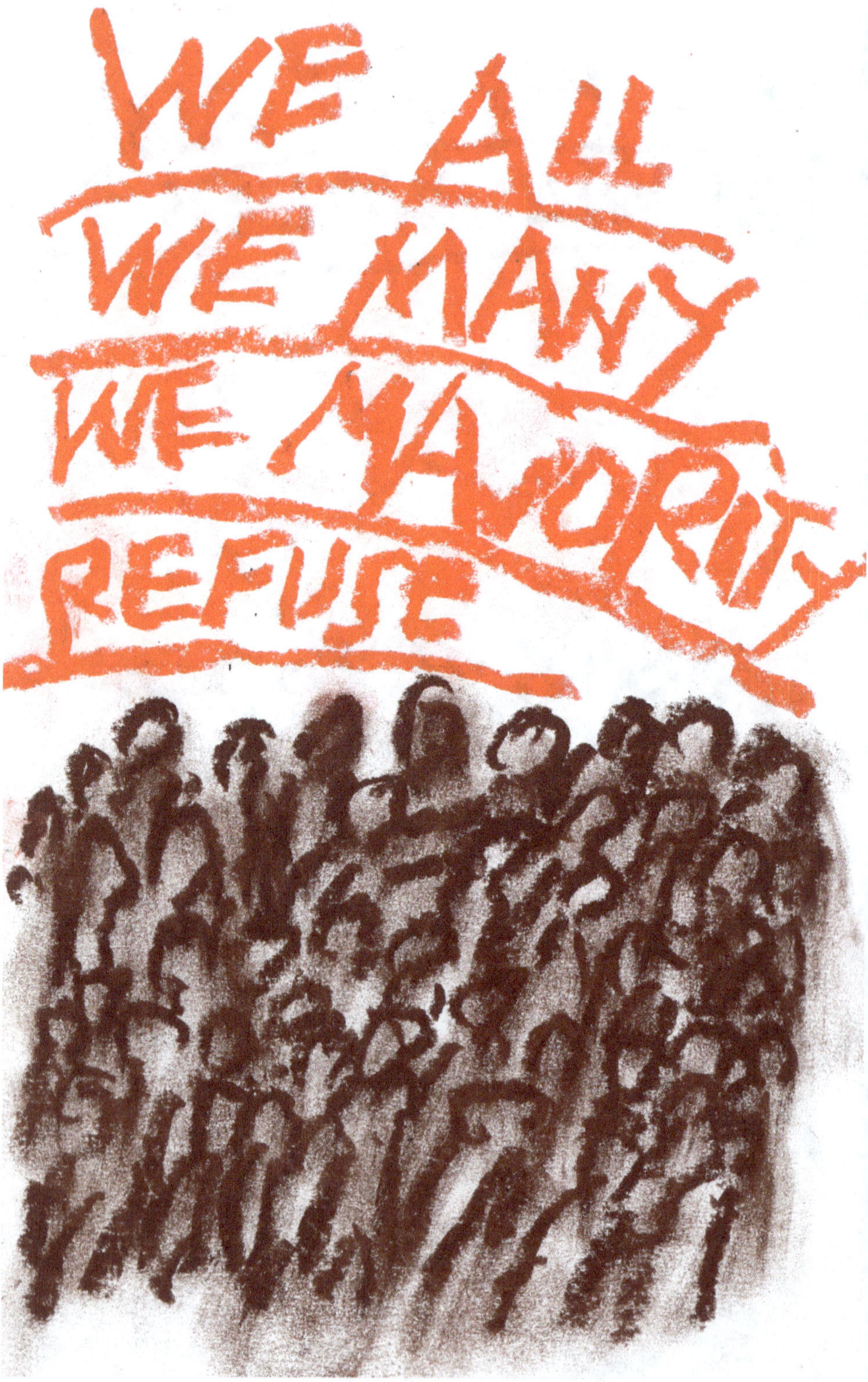

WE ALL
WE MANY
WE MAJORITY
REFUSE

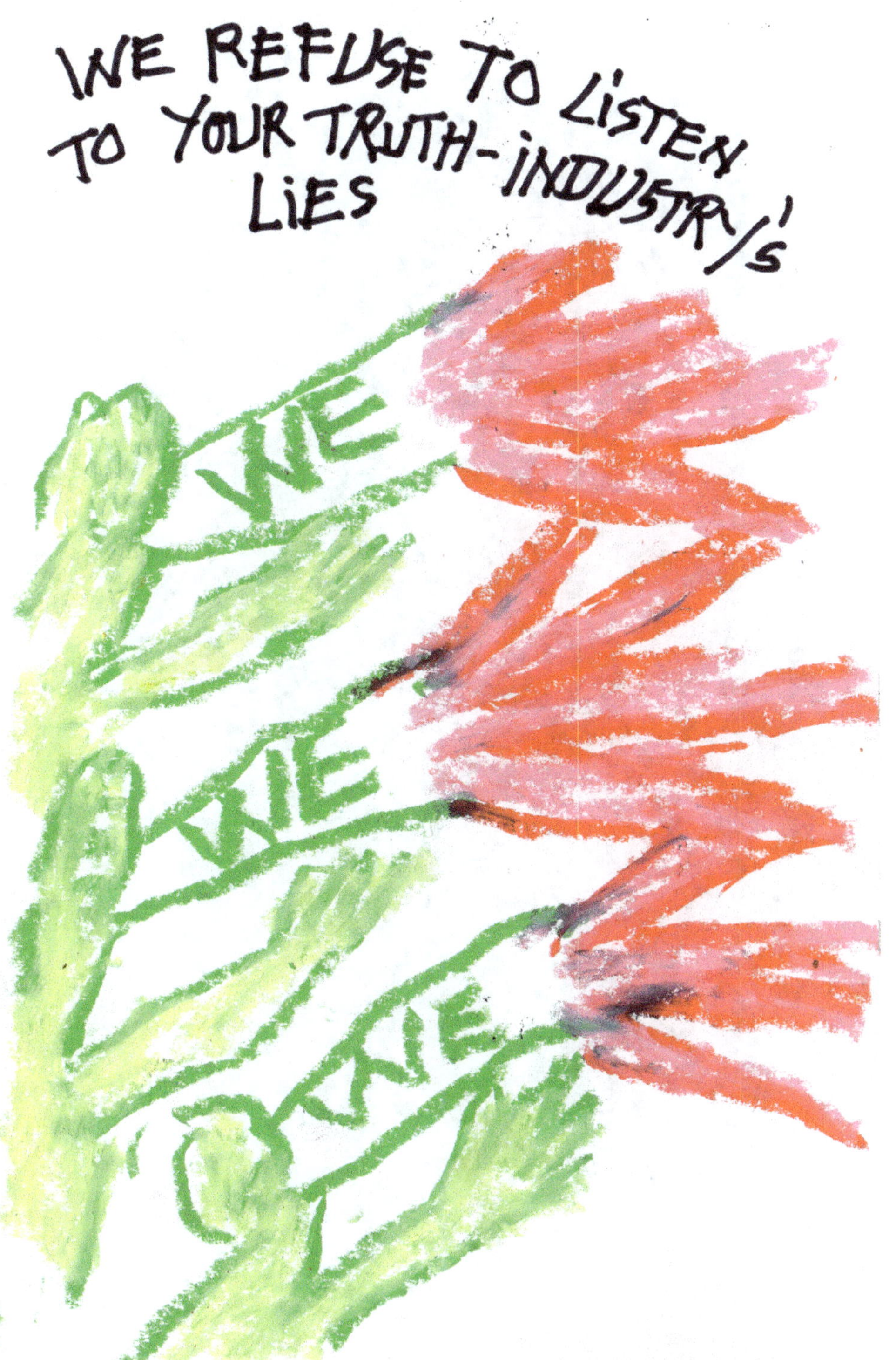
WE REFUSE TO LISTEN
TO YOUR TRUTH-INDUSTRY'S
LIES
WE
WE
WE

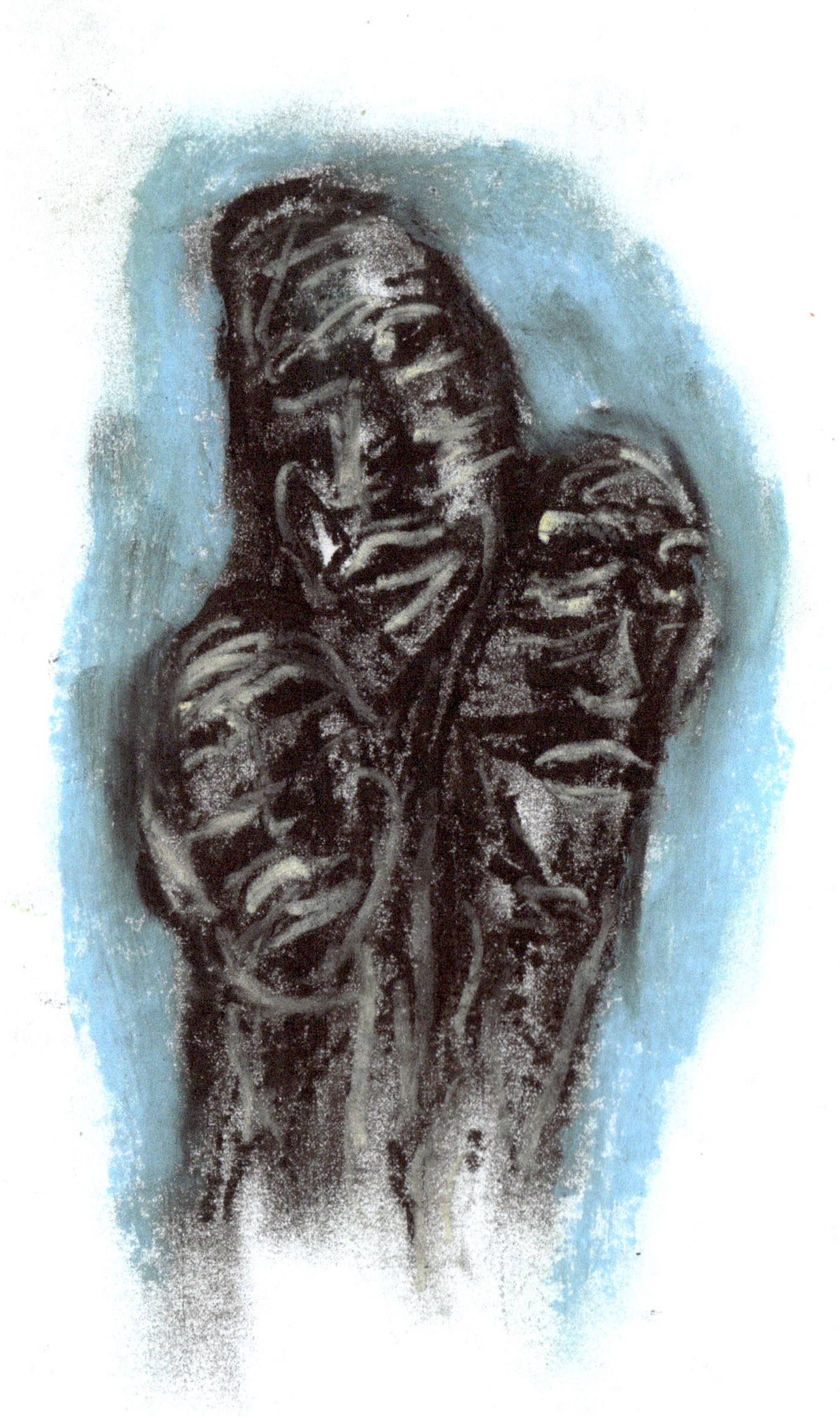

WE OUR MINDS
+ HEARTS + BODIES
REFUSE TO SERVE THIS
MASSMURDERING EMPIRE

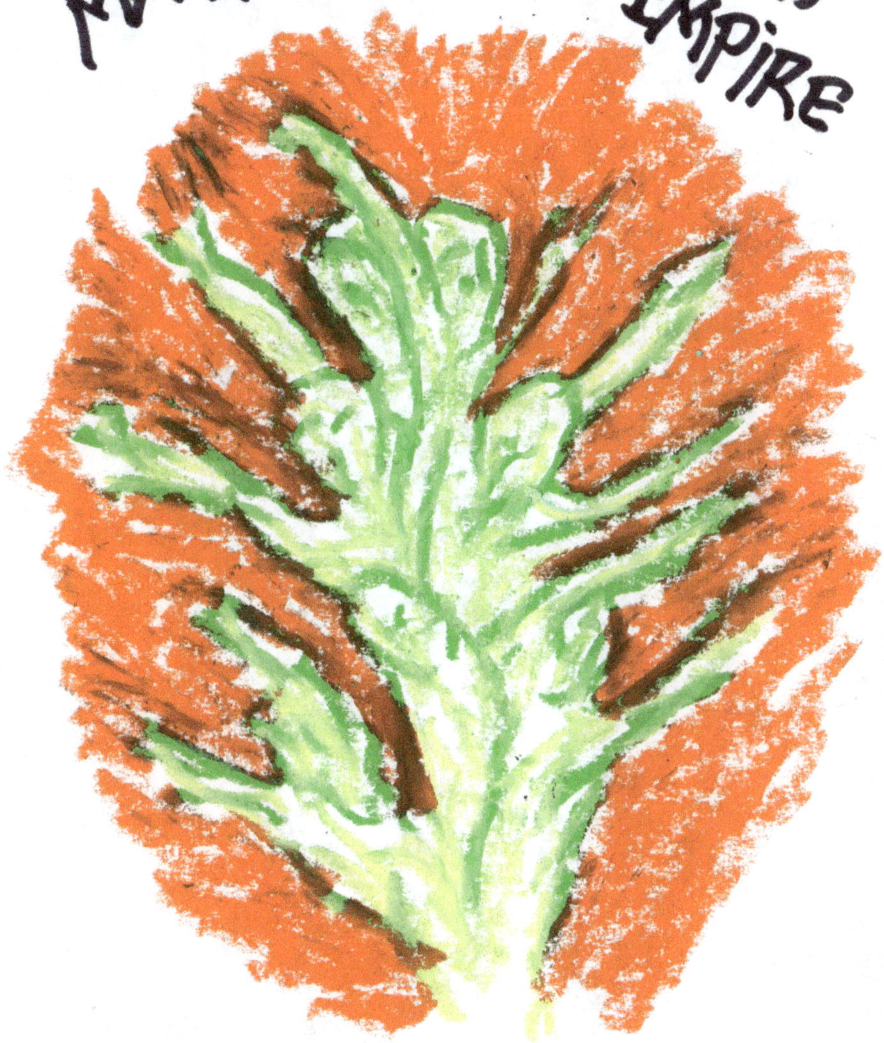

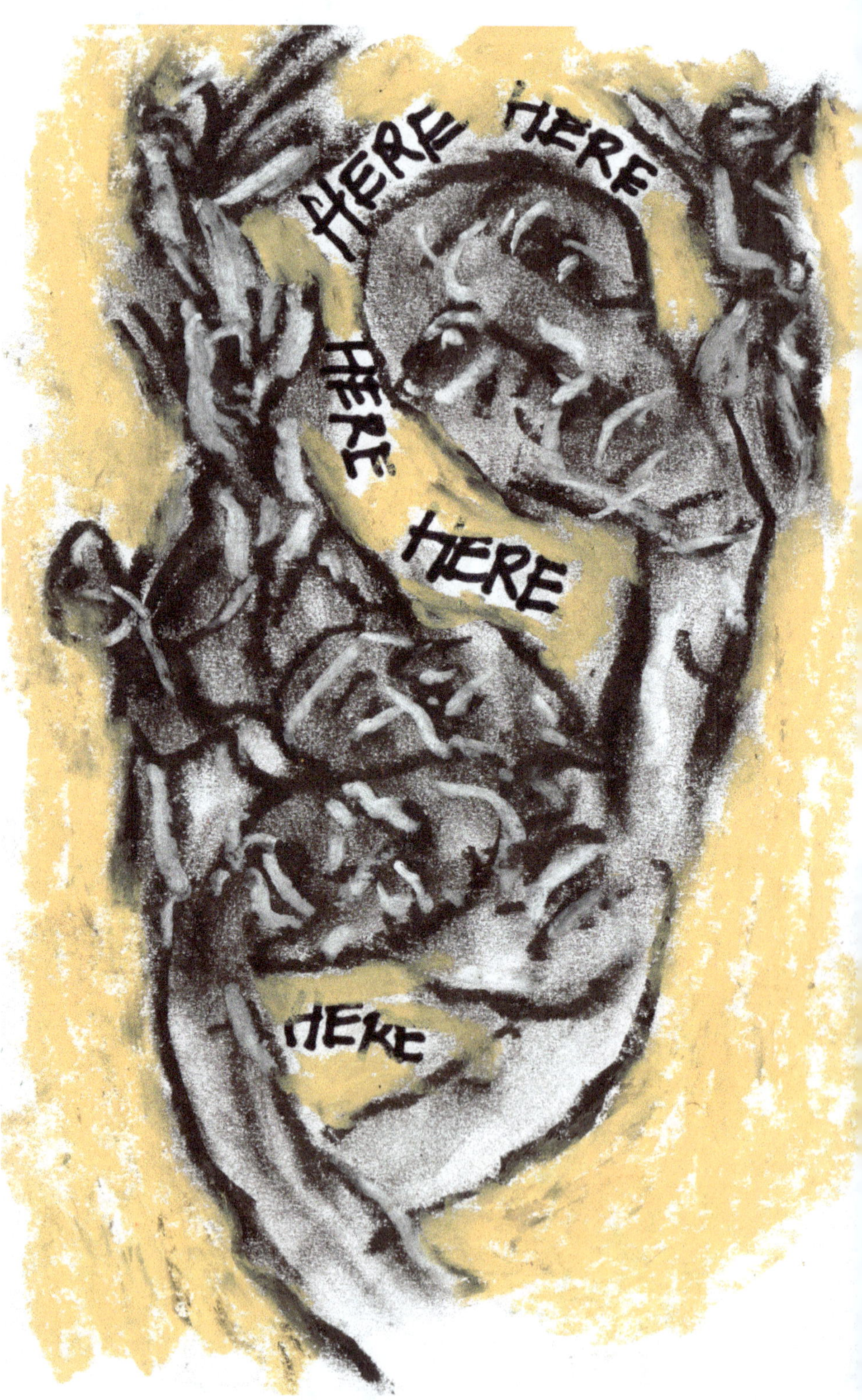

HERE HERE
HERE
HERE
HERE

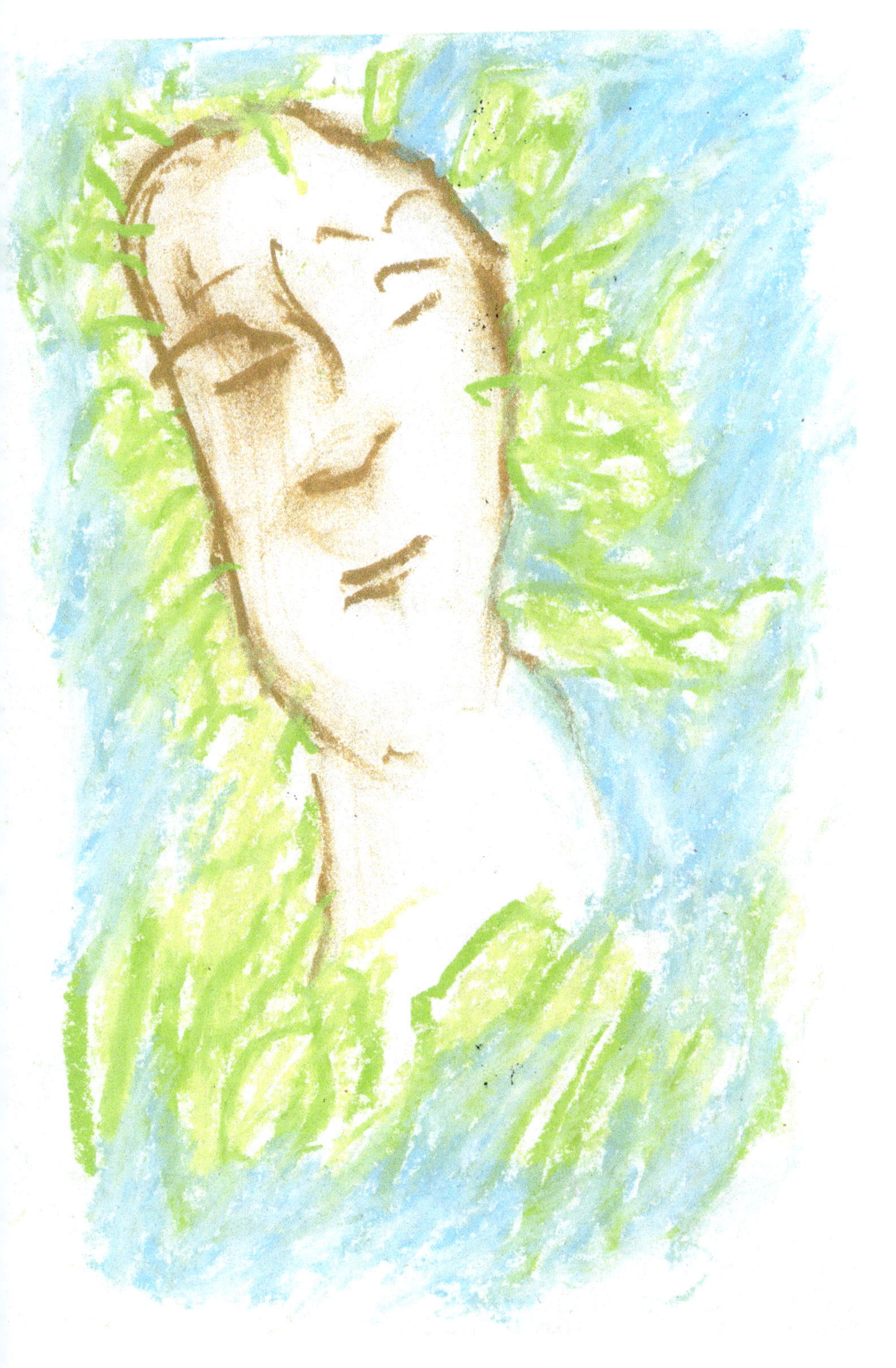

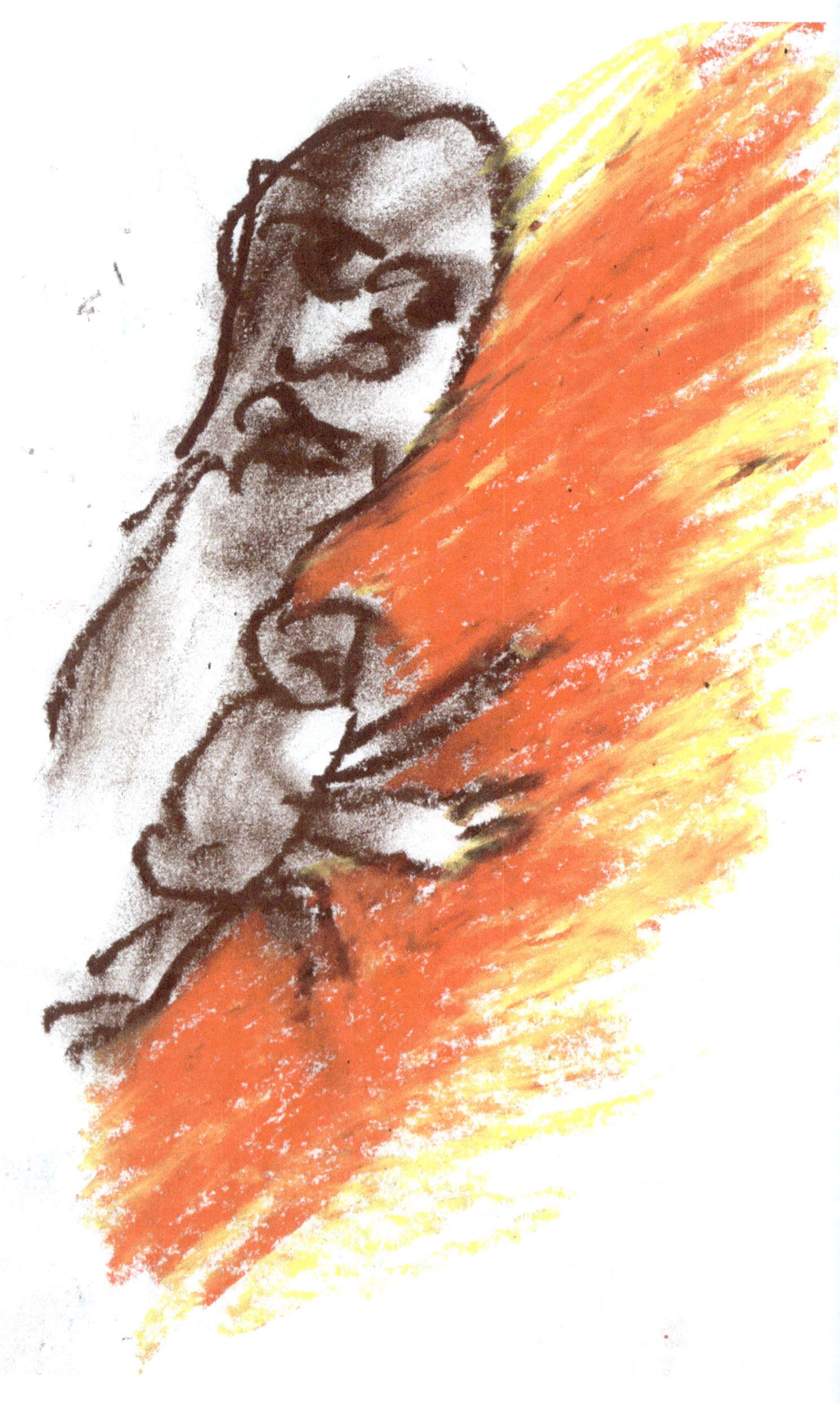

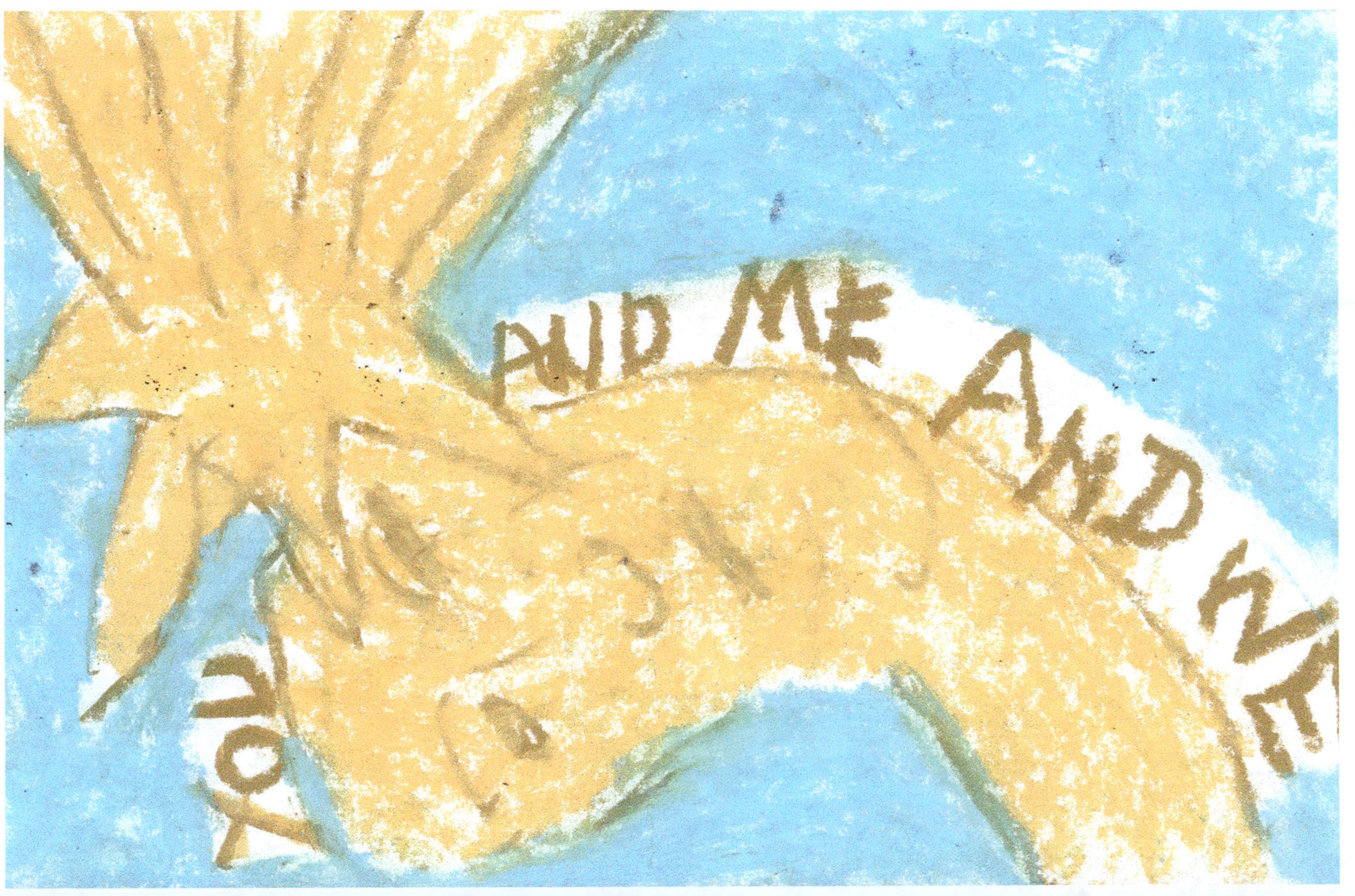
YOU
AND ME AND WE

WE
POSSIBILITAR-
iANS
[MUST]

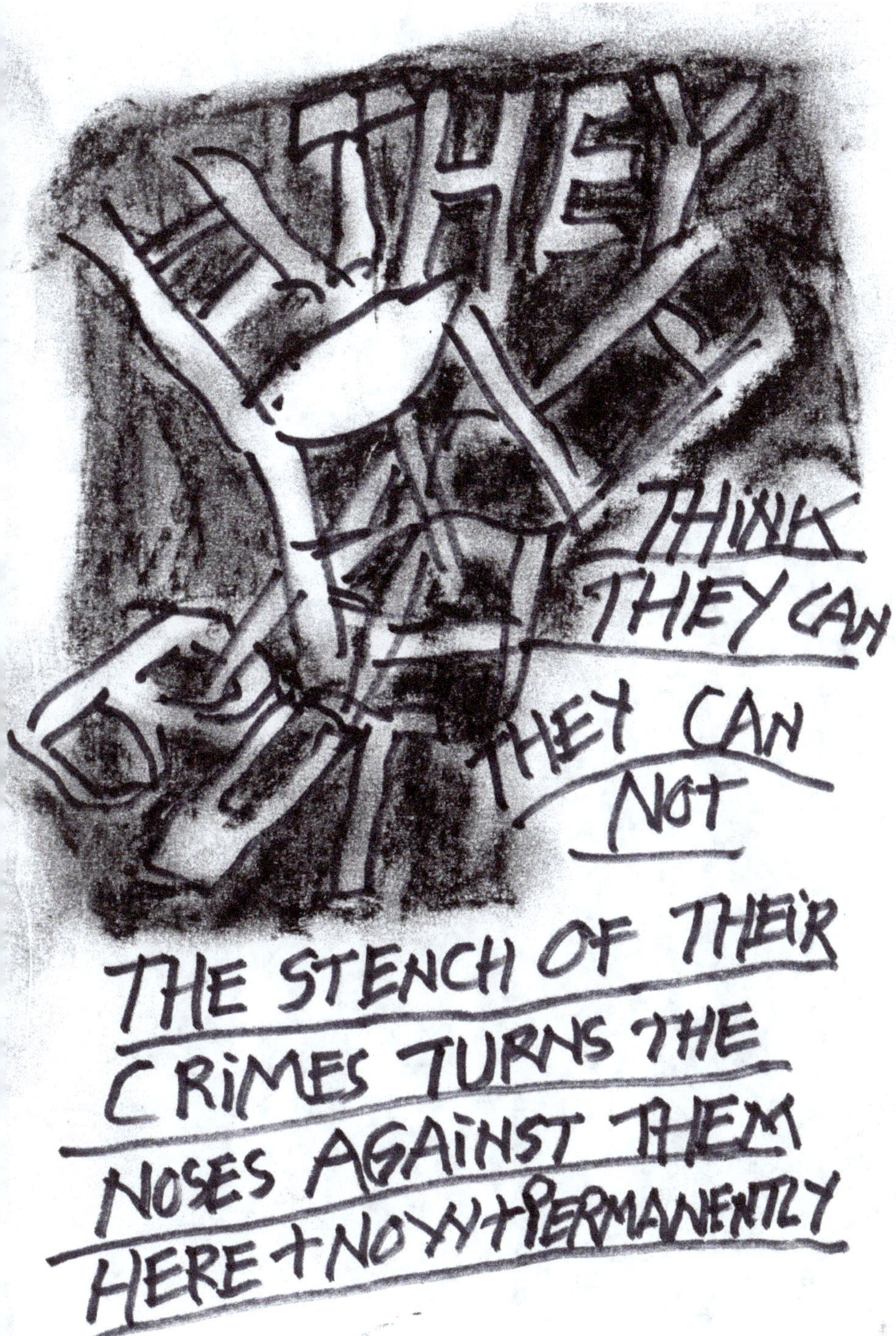

THEY
THINK
THEY CAN
THEY CAN
NOT
THE STENCH OF THEIR
CRIMES TURNS THE
NOSES AGAINST THEM
HERE + NOW + PERMANENTLY

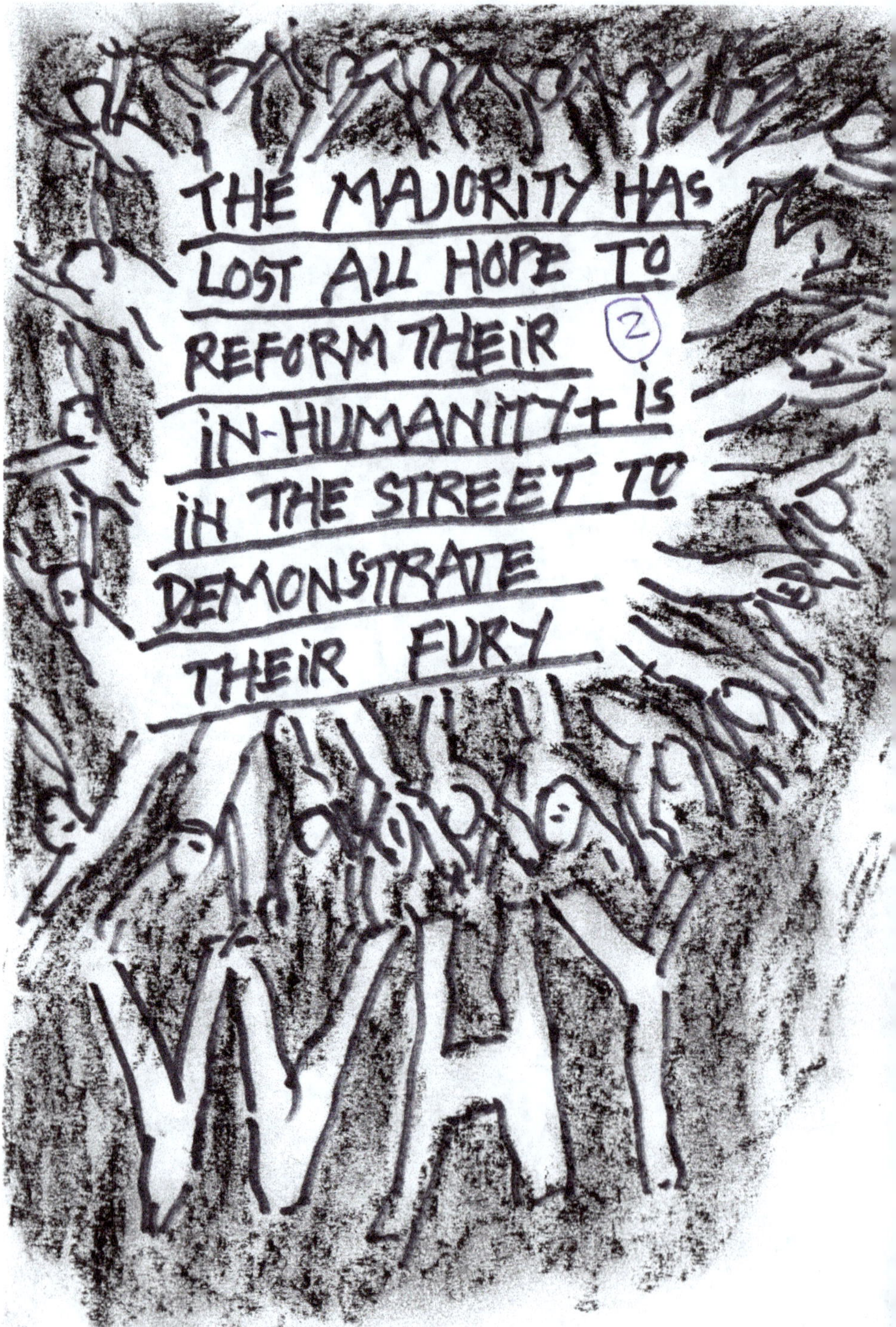

THE MAJORITY HAS
LOST ALL HOPE TO
REFORM THEIR (2)
IN-HUMANITY + IS
IN THE STREET TO
DEMONSTRATE
THEIR FURY
WHY

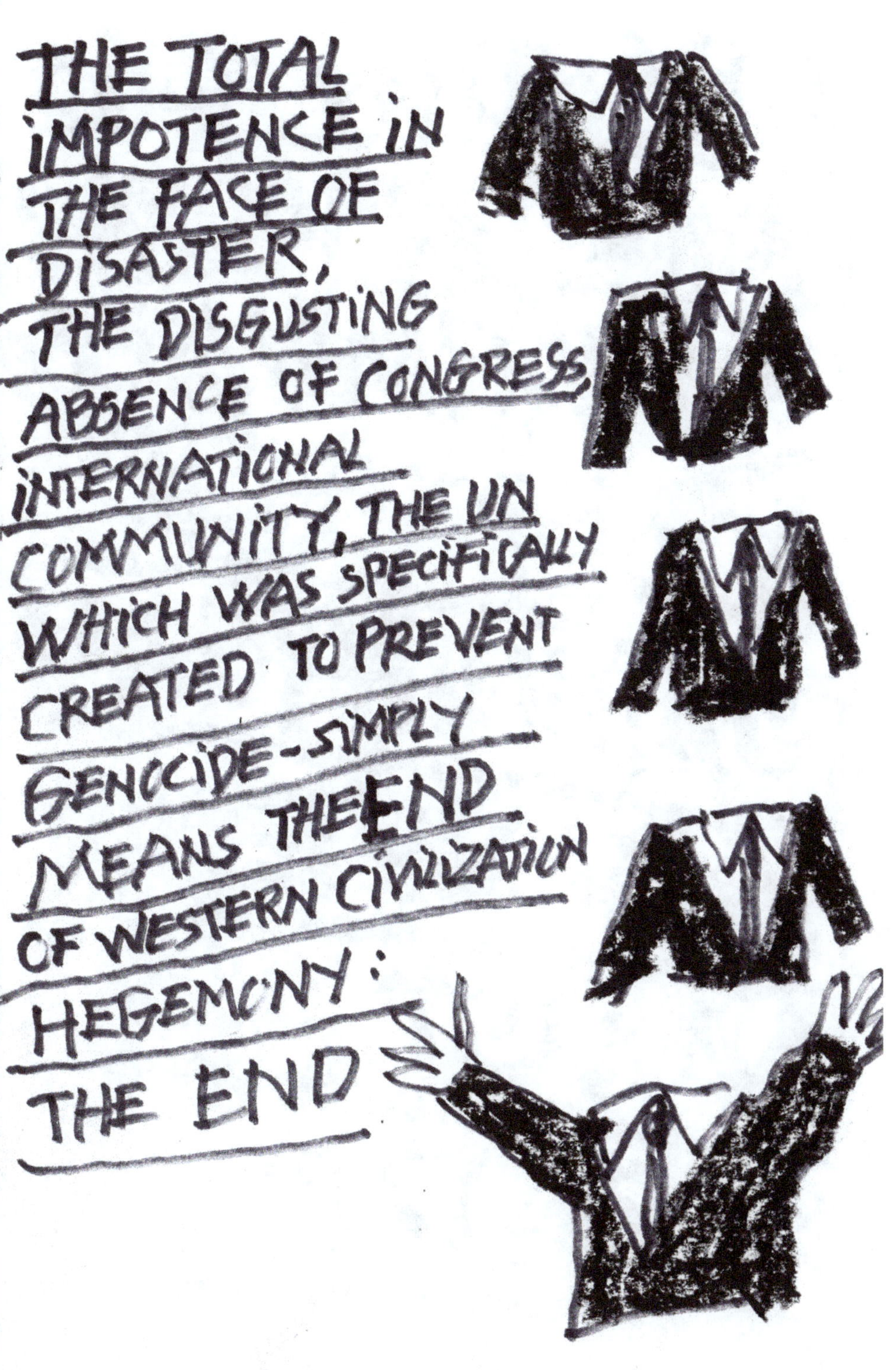

THE TOTAL IMPOTENCE IN THE FACE OF DISASTER, THE DISGUSTING ABSENCE OF CONGRESS, INTERNATIONAL COMMUNITY, THE UN WHICH WAS SPECIFICALLY CREATED TO PREVENT GENOCIDE - SIMPLY MEANS THE END OF WESTERN CIVILIZATION HEGEMONY:
THE END

ABANDON THIS
FAKE DEMOCRACY
OF WARMONGERS
ADOPT THE
POSSIBILITARIAN
YES WE
MUST
PARADE

UTOPIA IN THE
STREET: THROW
SHIT AT THE
REPRESENTATIVES
OF FALSEHOOD.
THE ORIGINAL
WHOLE OF
MOTHER DIRT
WHO MAKES

+ UNMAKES
US REQUIRES
OUR OPPOSITION
TO THE
OBVIOUS
EVIL OF
THE
SYSTEM

WE
POSSIBILITARIAN
BIRDS

MUST

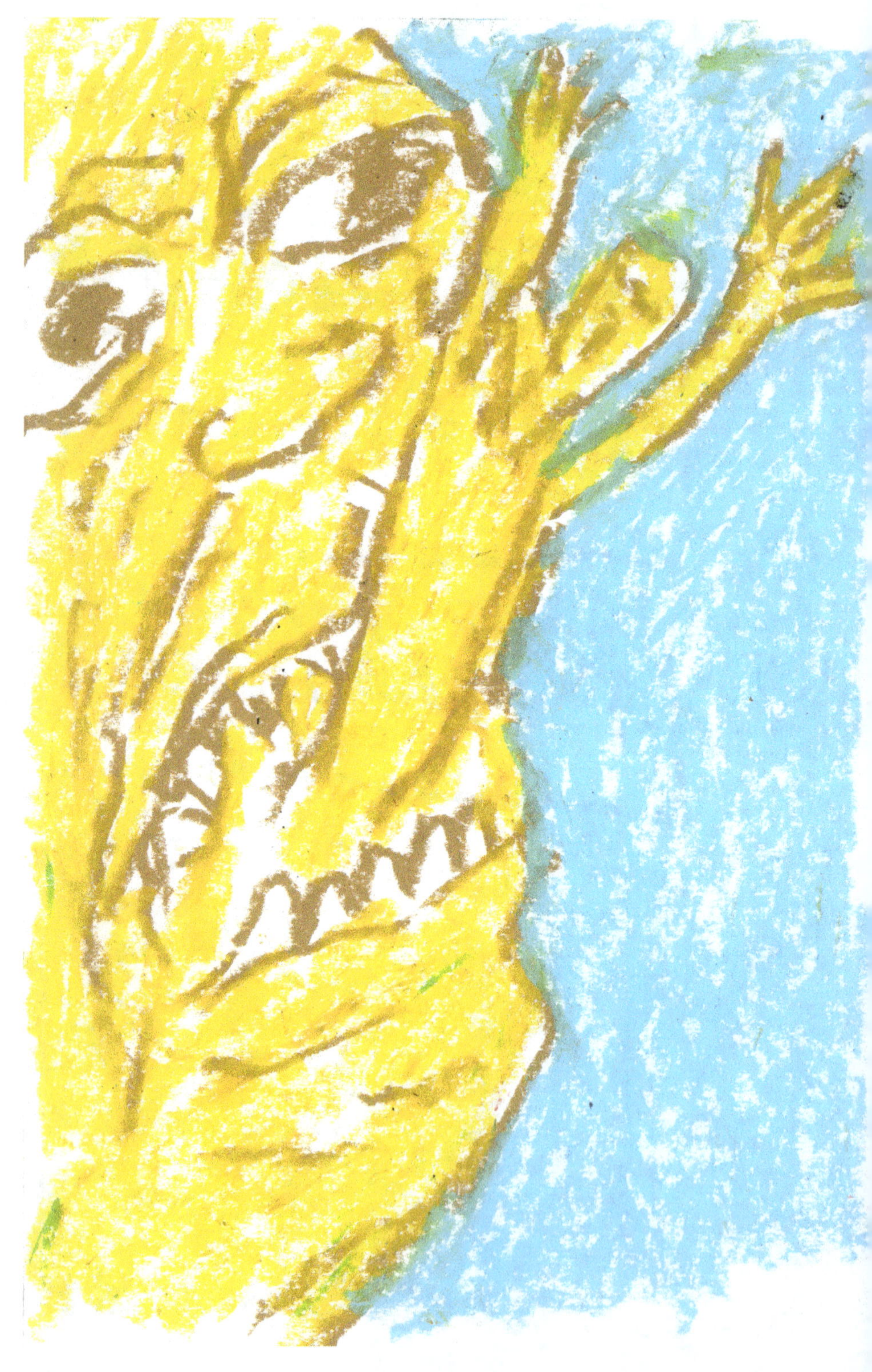

WHICH LUST FOR LIFE. IS LEFT IN THE EARTHLING WHO IS BORN WITH THE LUST FOR LIFE

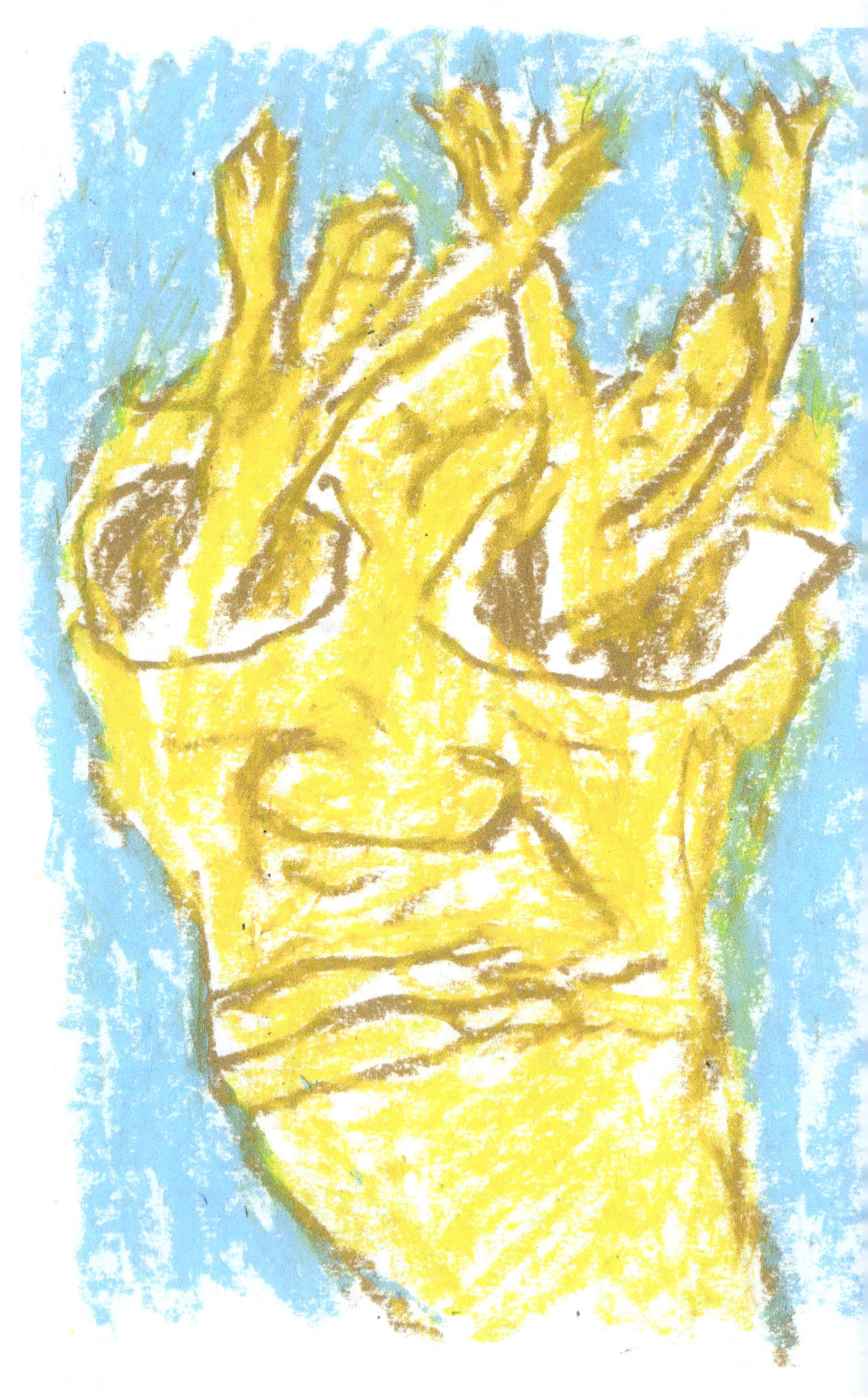

TAKEN AWAY BY THE INSTITUTION-ALIZED KILLERS OF ANOTHER EQUALLY GIFTED LIFE + CAN ONLY BE RESTORED BY PRACTICING SOLIDARITY WITH THAT OTHER LIFE

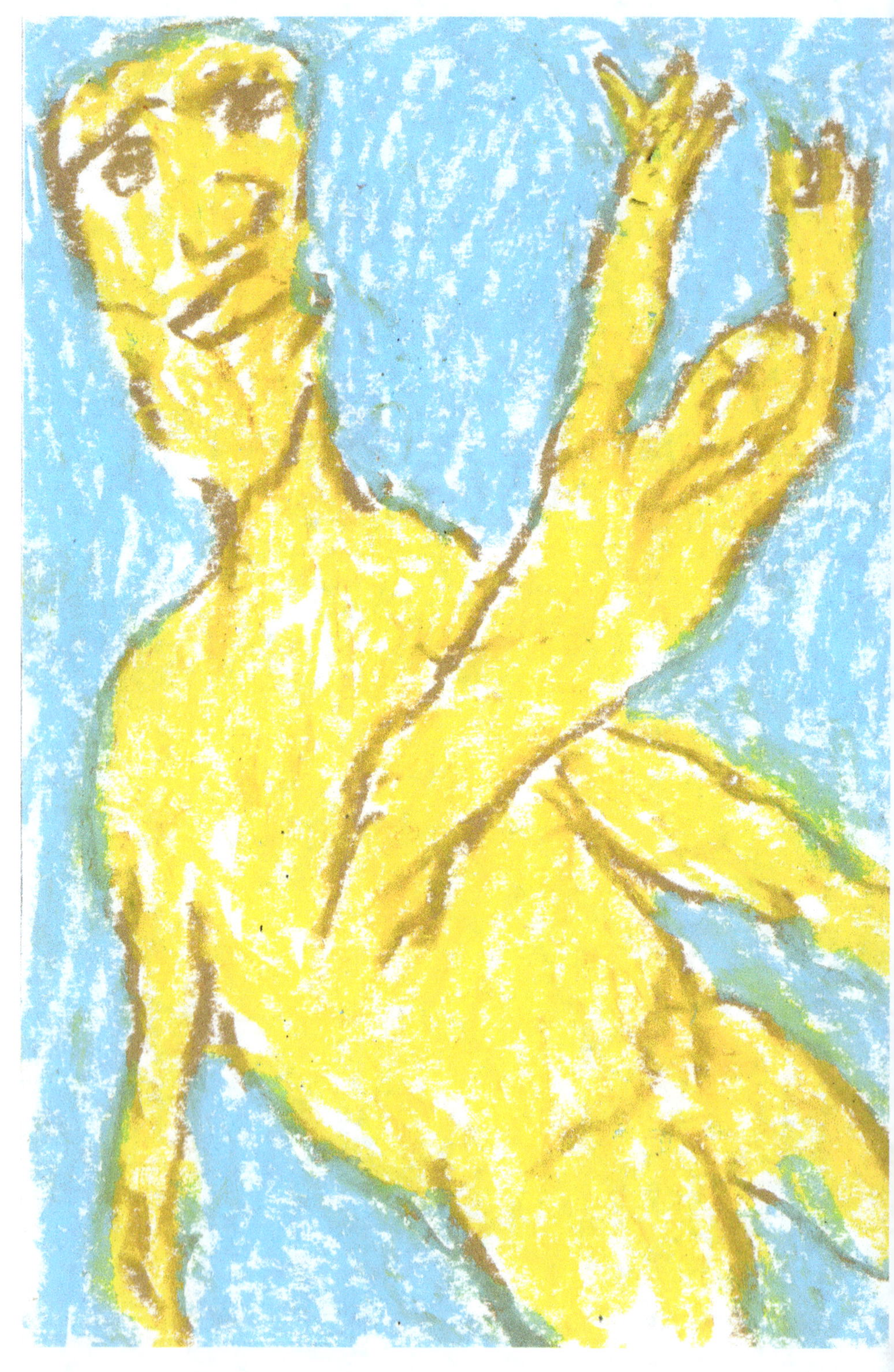

ONLY WE THE MAJORITY UNDERNEATH THE MAJORITY

CAN DO THE RESTORING

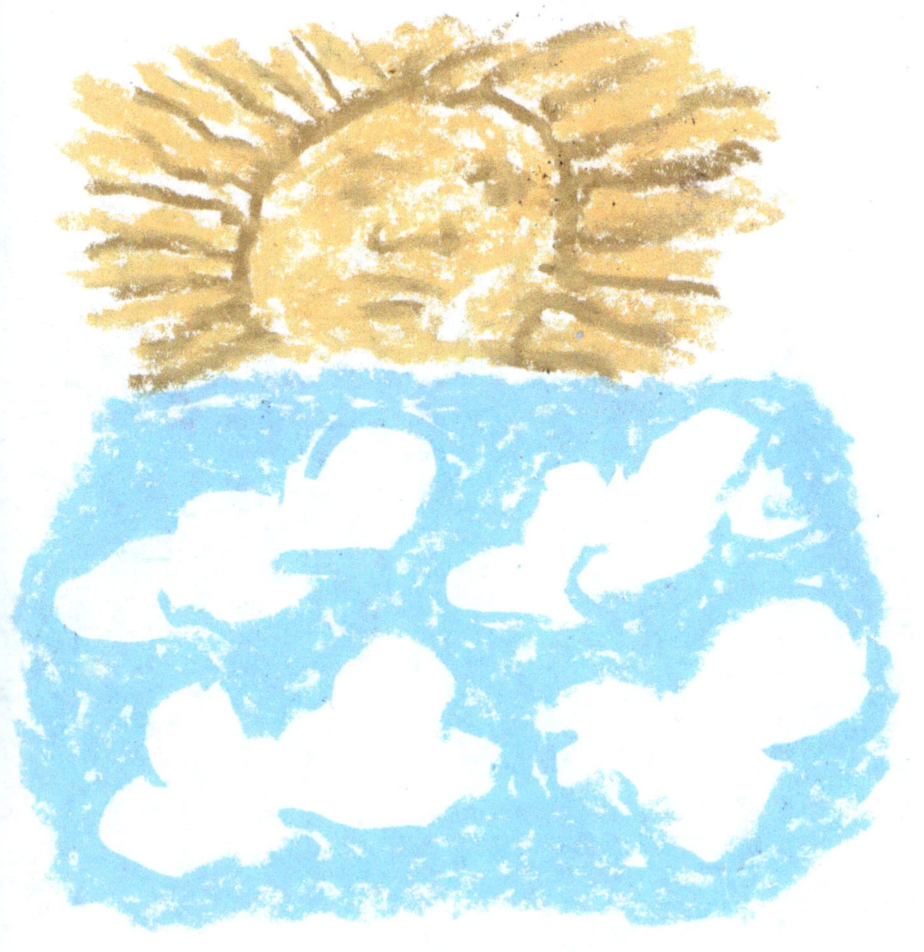

BY FLYING
WHITE BIRD
FLOCKS + THEIR
YELLS THROUGH
THE CITY

YELLS OF UN-
PRECEDENTED
INTENSITY

WHERE? RIGHT HERE!
NOW

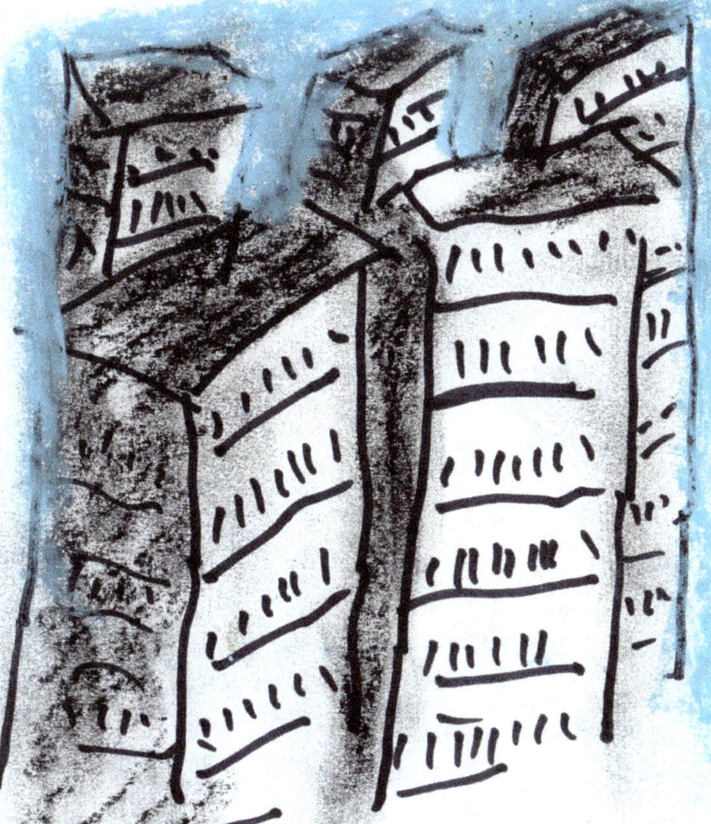

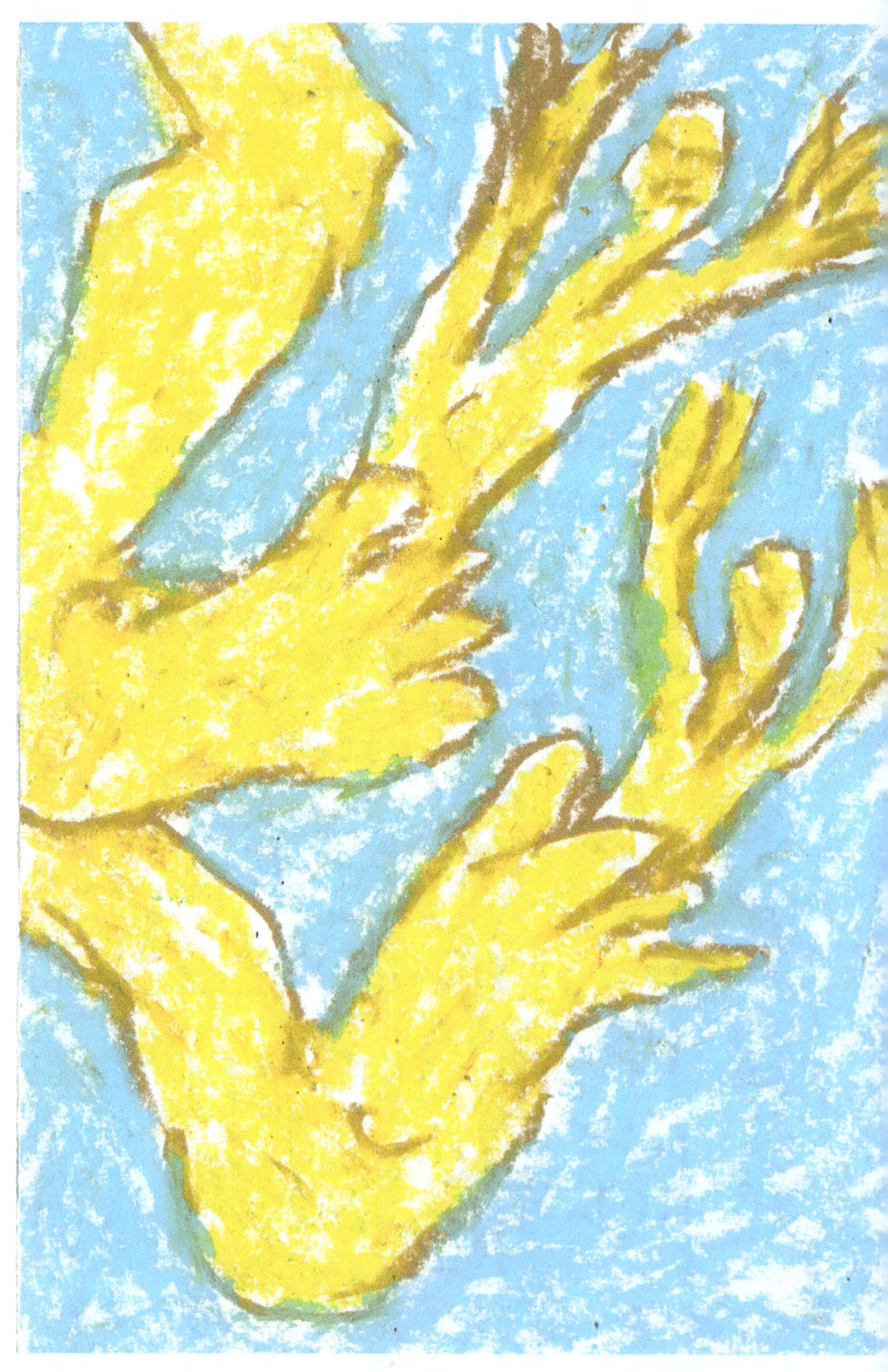

VIVE POSSIBILITARIAN

JUBILATIONISTS

WHERE

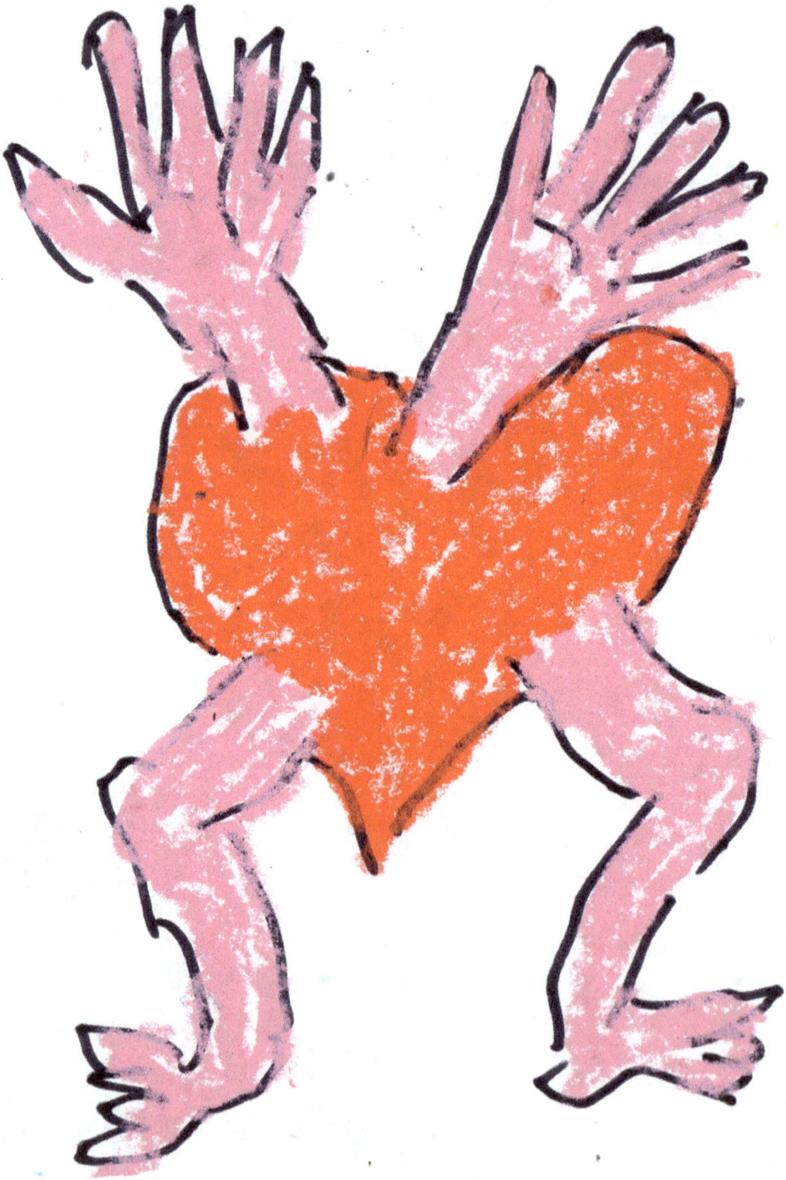

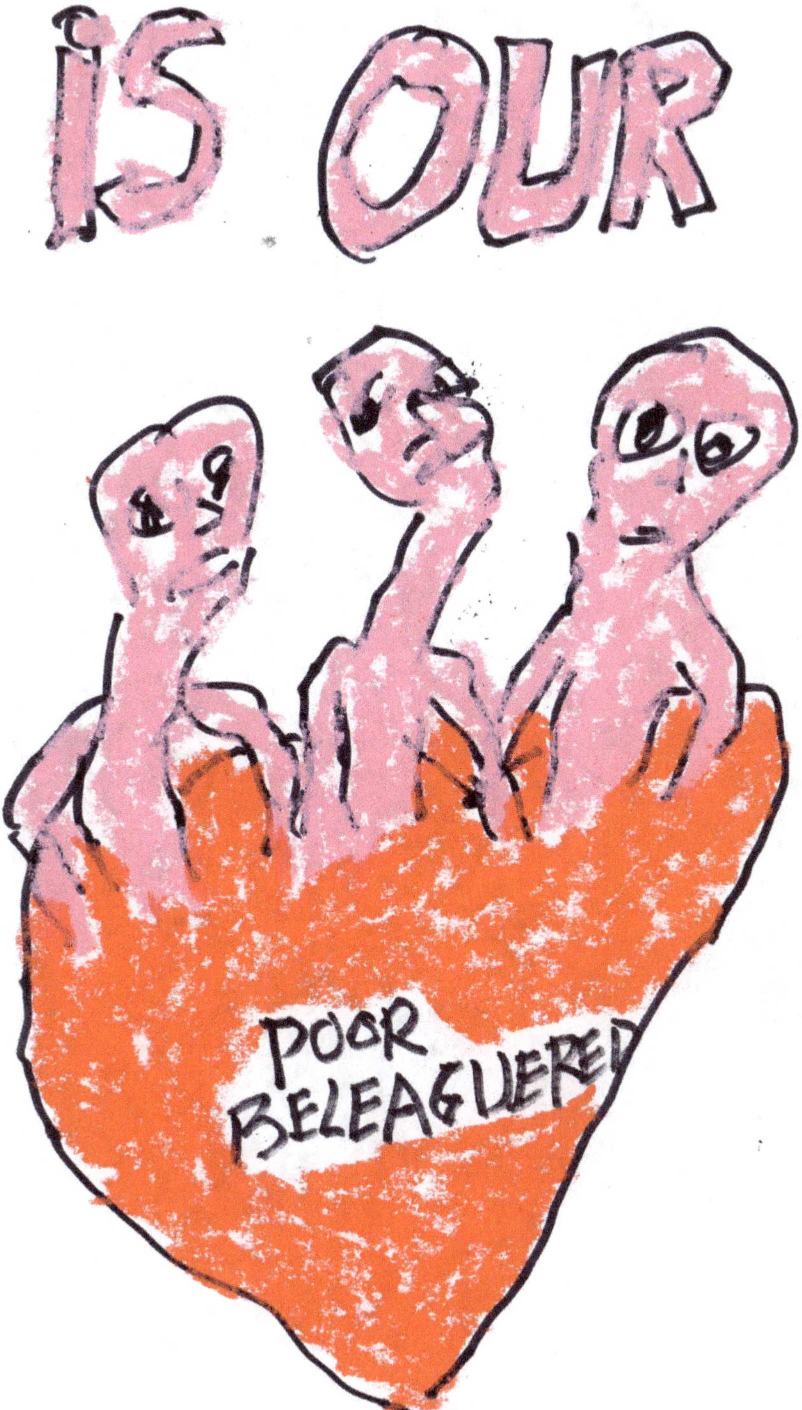

IS OUR
POOR BELEAGUERED

THE ONE

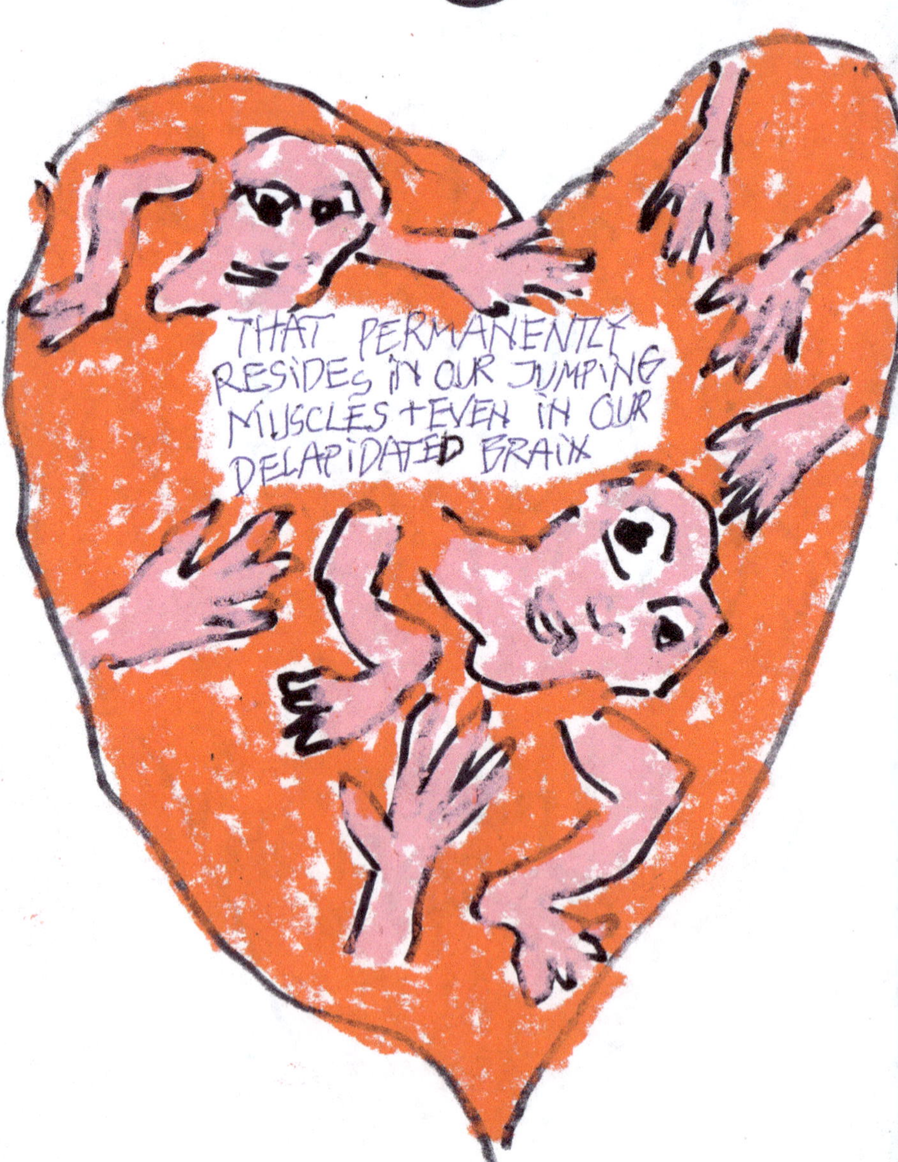

THAT PERMANENTLY RESIDES IN OUR JUMPING MUSCLES + EVEN IN OUR DELAPIDATED BRAIN

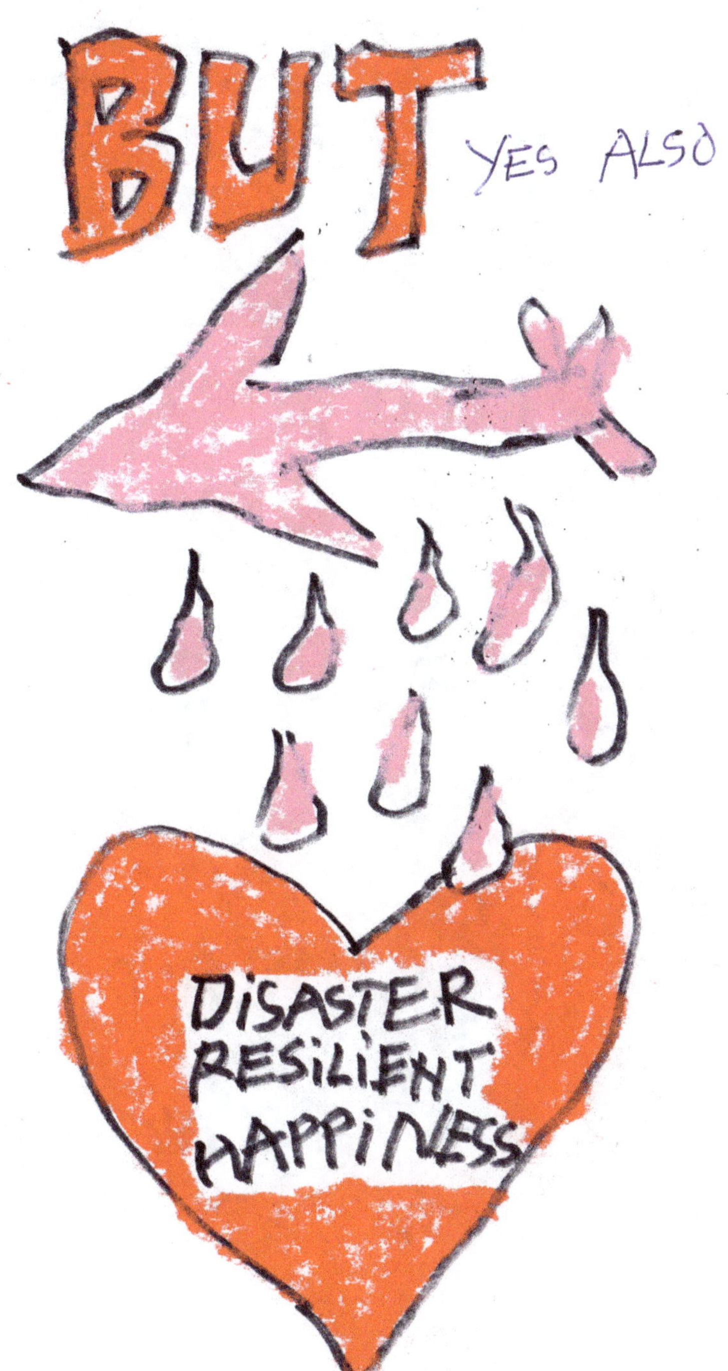

BUT
YES ALSO
DISASTER
RESILIENT
HAPPINESS

+ REFUSES TO GIVE UP
NO
NO
NO
NO

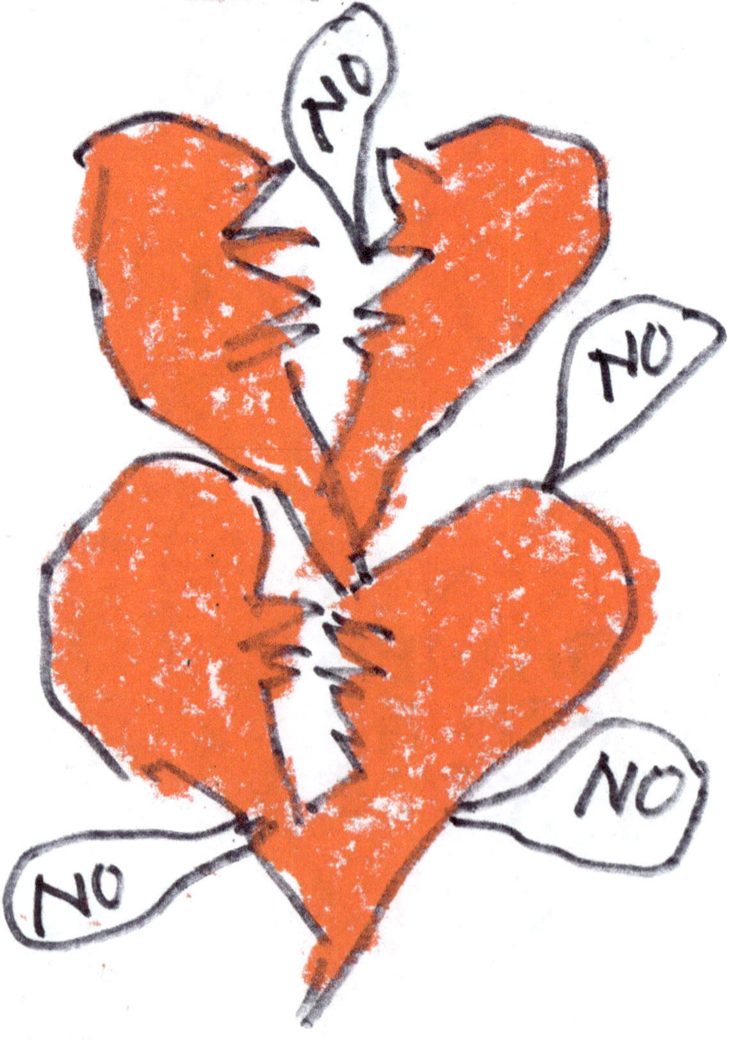

+ ASSERTS ITS PROMINENCE
OVER THE HEARTLESS
DILIGENTLY INSTALLED
UNHAPPINESS SYSTEM OF
THE MASSMURDERERS

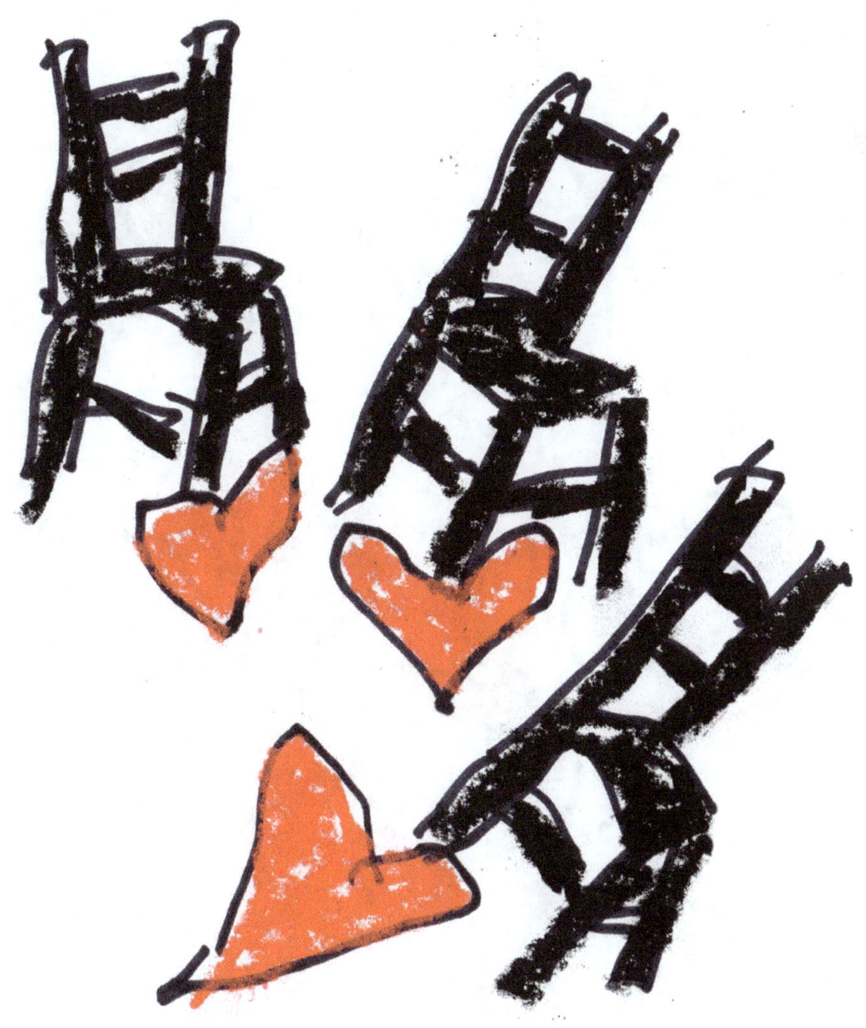

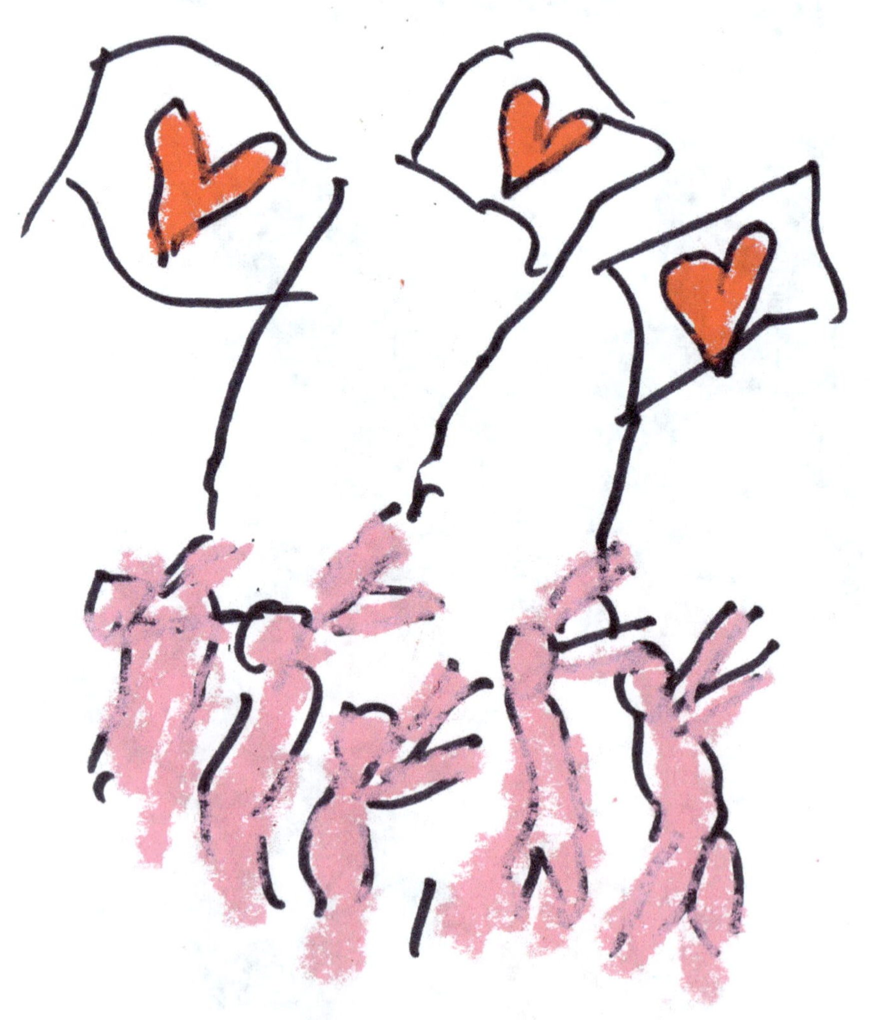
AND
TAKES TO THE
STREETS OF EVERYWHERE

AND + JUBILATES
ITS RIDICULOUS JUBILATIONS
AGAINST

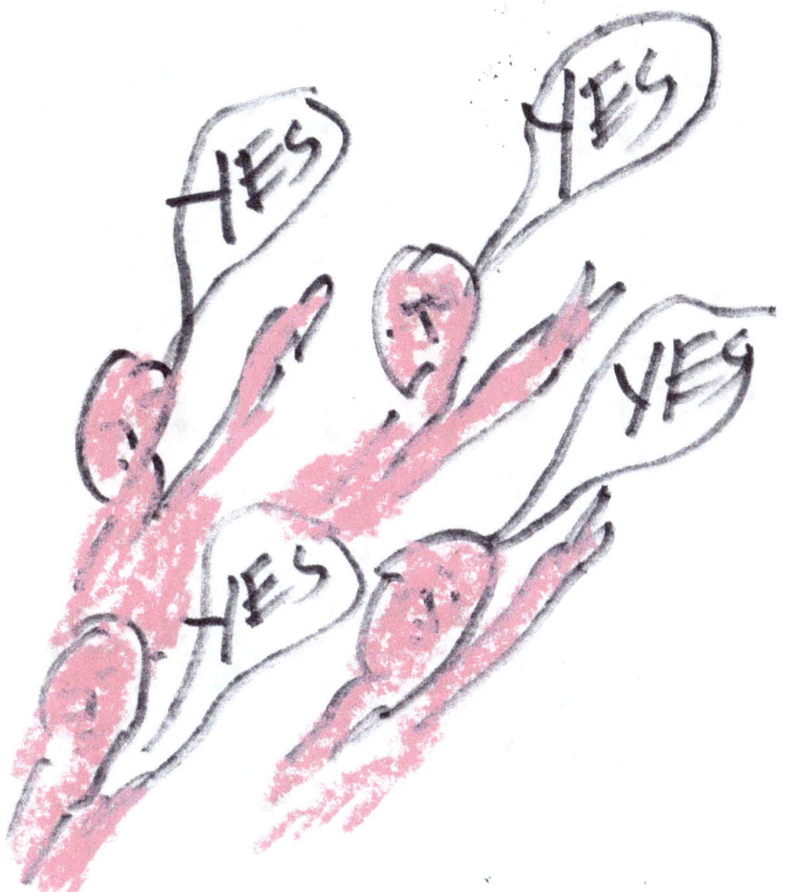

THE MASSIVE
AMOUNTS OF UNNECESSARY
PAIN

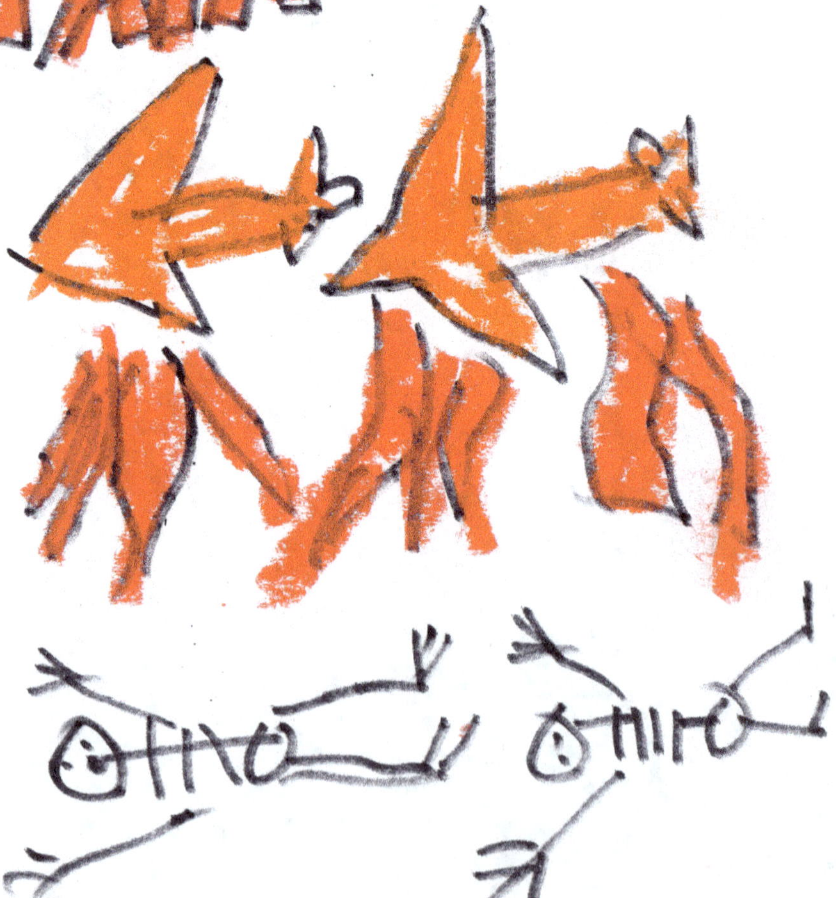

AND DANCE STILL THE NORTHEAST KINGDOM SNOWFLAKES DANCE TO ITS BEAT

WE POSSIBILITARIANS

GENOCIDERS BEWARE

THE

NEVER-MIND END-OF-THE-ROAD
TYPICAL DWARF OF THE
GIANT SYSTEM

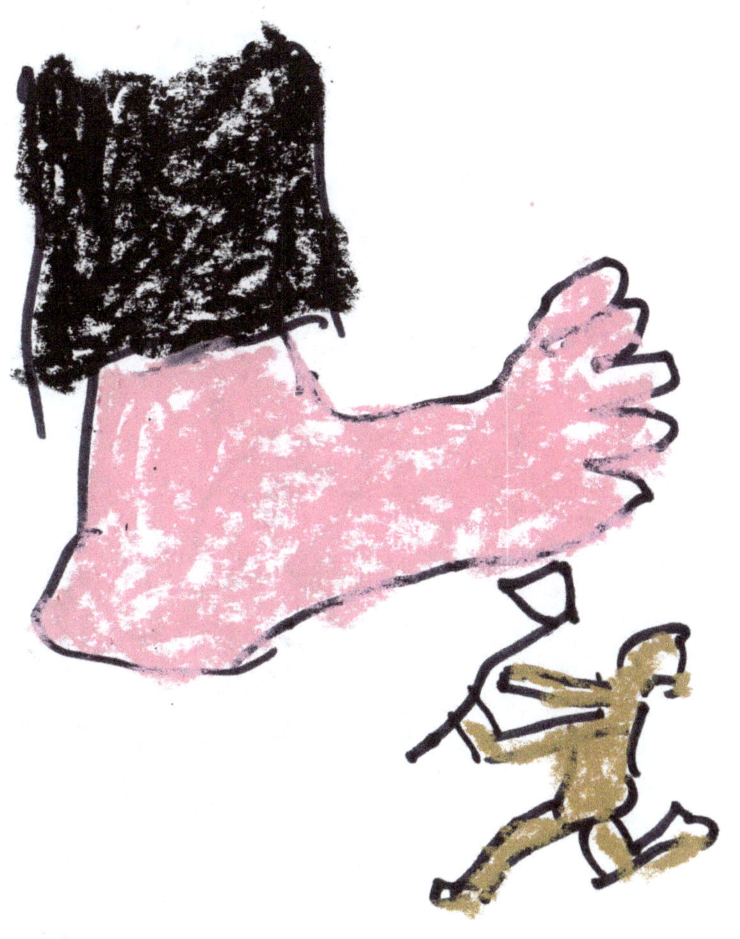

AIMS TO BE

OF SERVICE TO FELLOW DWARVES
WHO MAY NOT HAVE HAD A CHANCE
TO CONSIDER THE RIDICULOUS
SENSATION OF ALL DWARF MATTERS

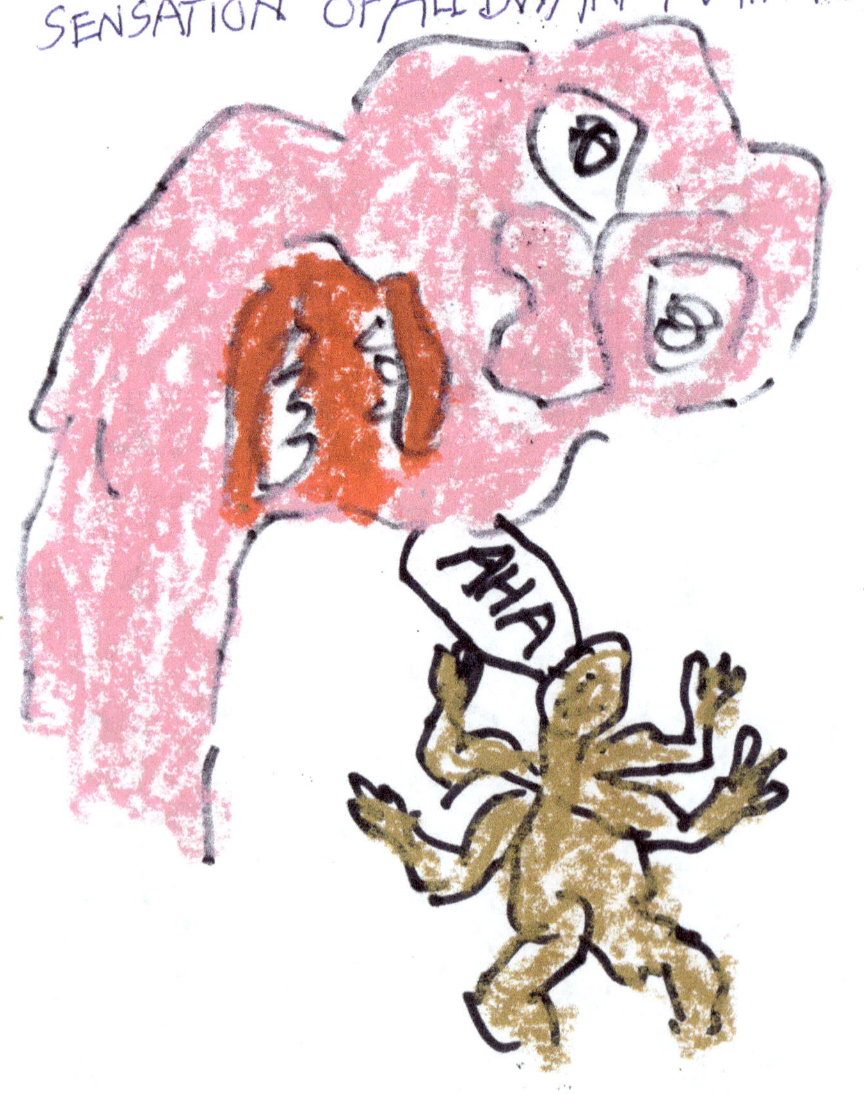

AND THEREFORE
MAY UNNECESSARILY SUFFER
THE GIANT SYSTEM OPPRESSIONS

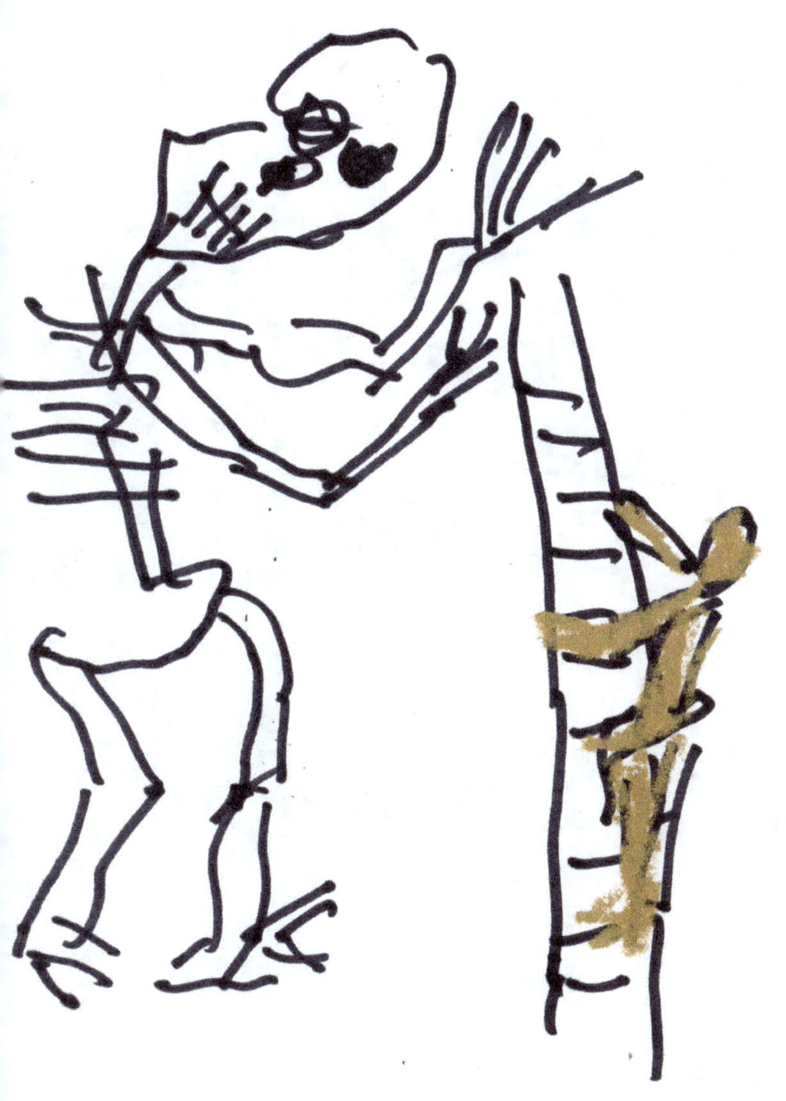

HOWEVER THAT
MAY BE: DWARVES ARE HERE
TO STAY WHEREAS GIANTS ARE
DOOMED AS A RESULT OF THEIR
OVERSIZE

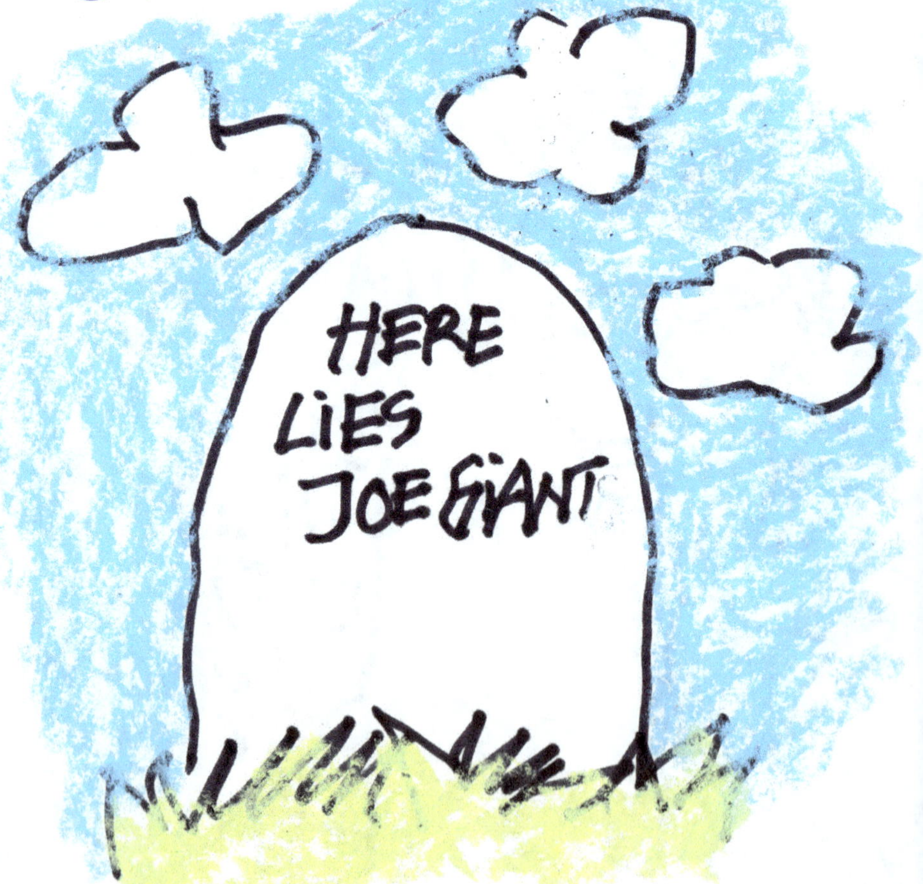

PRECISELY THE
MINIATURE MEANS OF PRODUCTION:
DESK, CHAIR, PAPER, PEN, LANGUAGE,
ALL DOWNSIZED TO THE APPROPRIATE
SIZE FOR THE DECREPIST MOMENT
FACILITATE THE SECRET ASPECTS OF
DWARFDOM

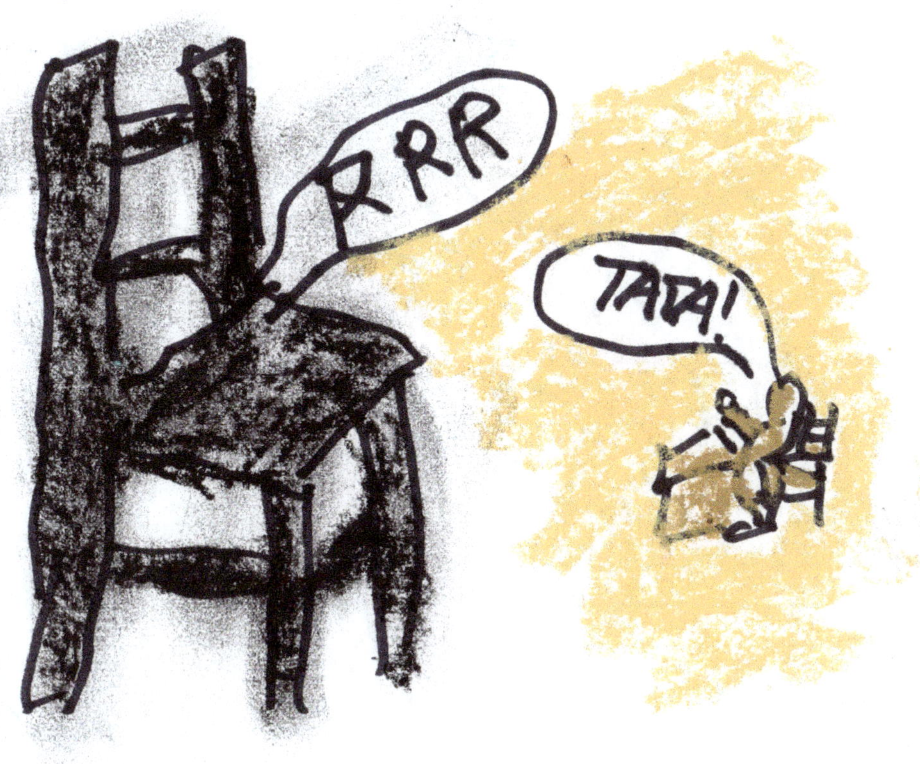

AVOID BULK
+ SURPLUS +CONSEQUENTLY
PRODUCE MORE SENSE OF THE NON-
SENSICAL KIND FOR THE ACTUAL
HEART-OF-THE MATTER TRUTH
INGREDIENT

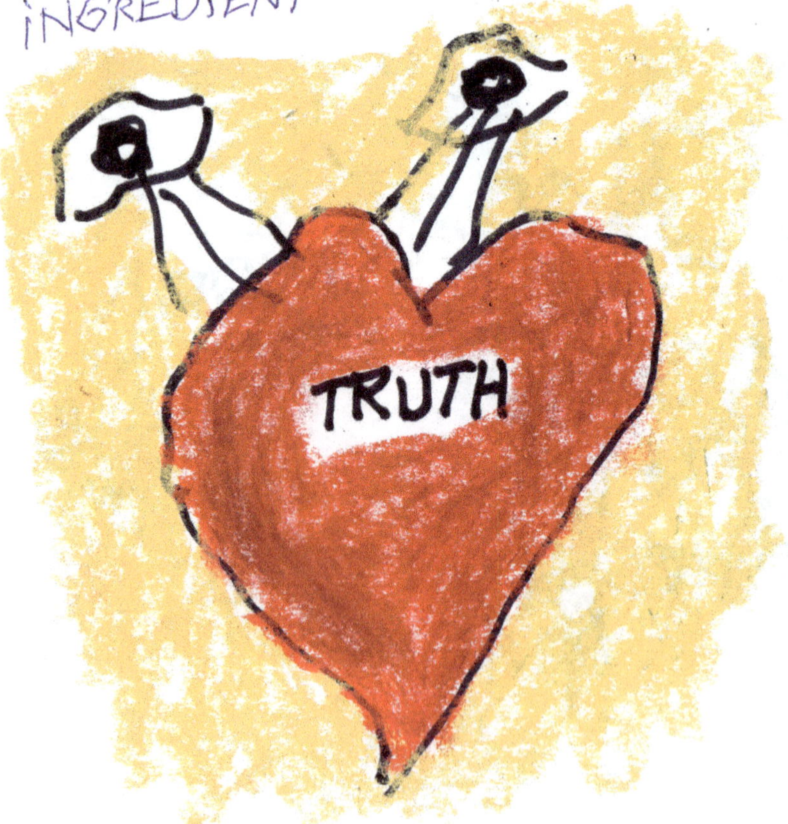

✝ THEREFORE FELLOW DWARVES

PRAISE the END-OF-THE-ROAD
NONSENSE + SENSE ALIKE + MAKE
IT SHINE LIKE THE SPARK THAT
LIGHTS YOUR CIGARBUTT

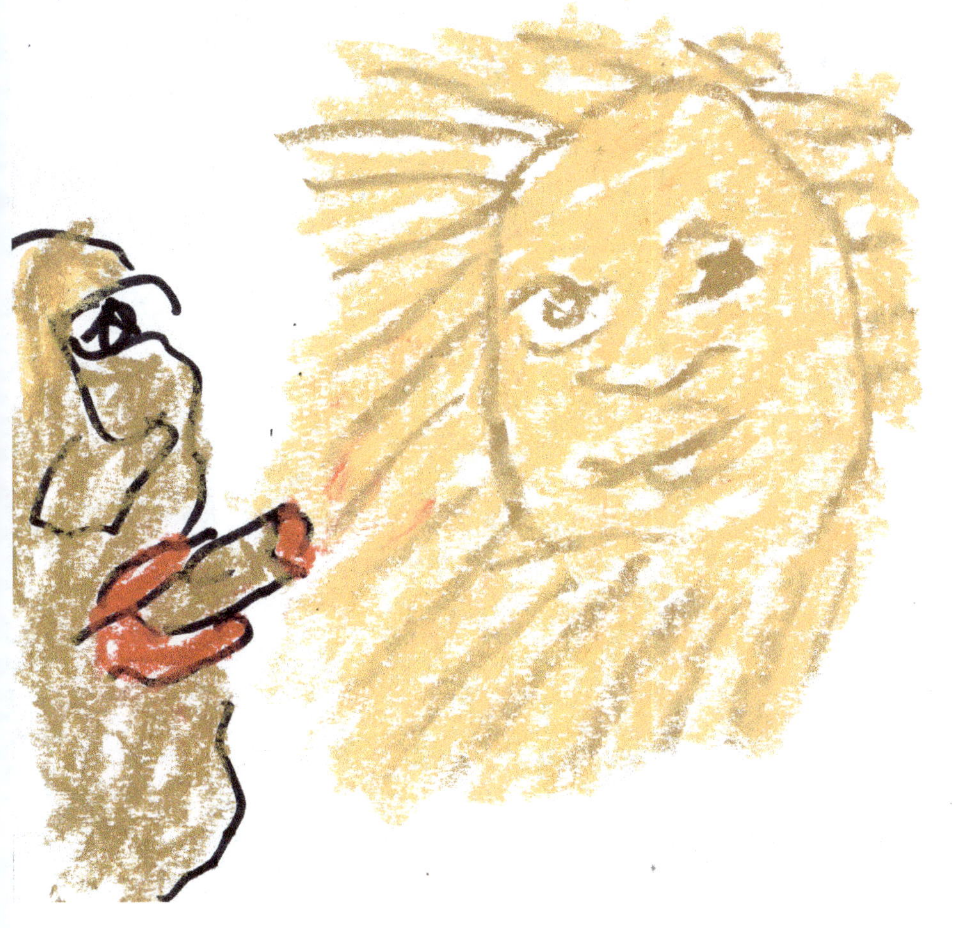

WE POSSIBILITAR-IANS

THE SUN RISES AND VOLUNTEERS ITS SERVICES TO THE NOW

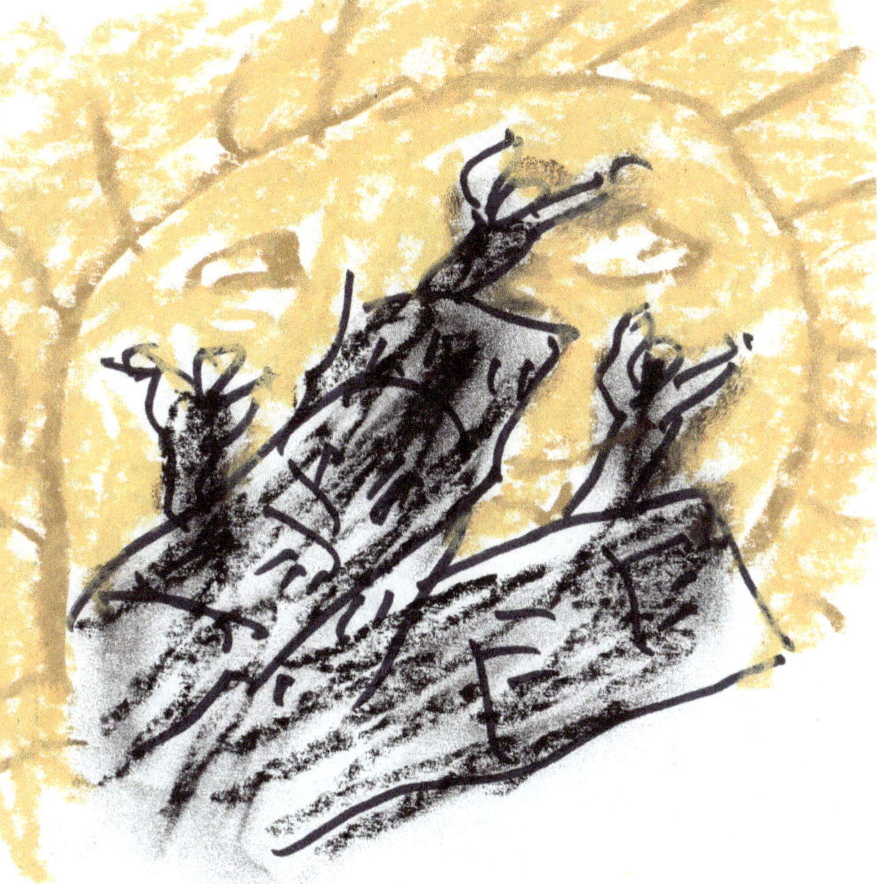

EVEN TO THE ABSURD NOW OF HUMANS WHO PRETEND TO BE EARTHLINGS

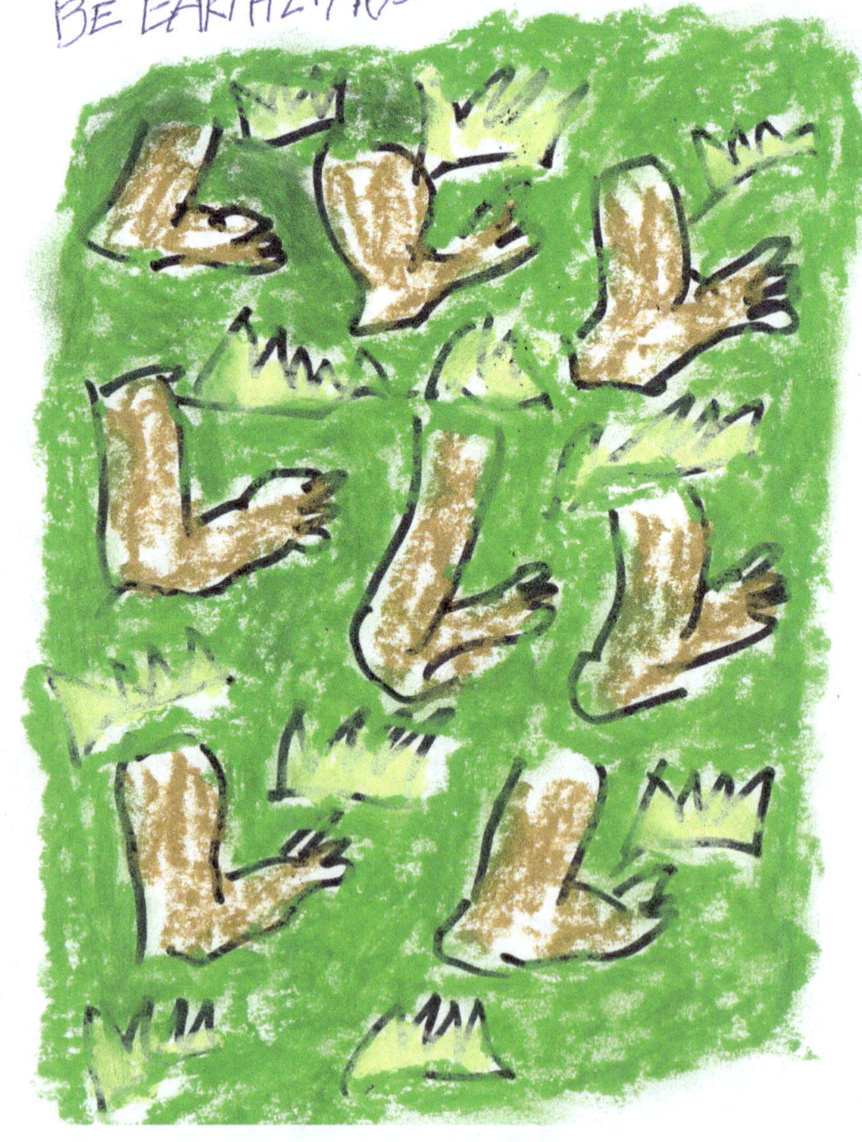

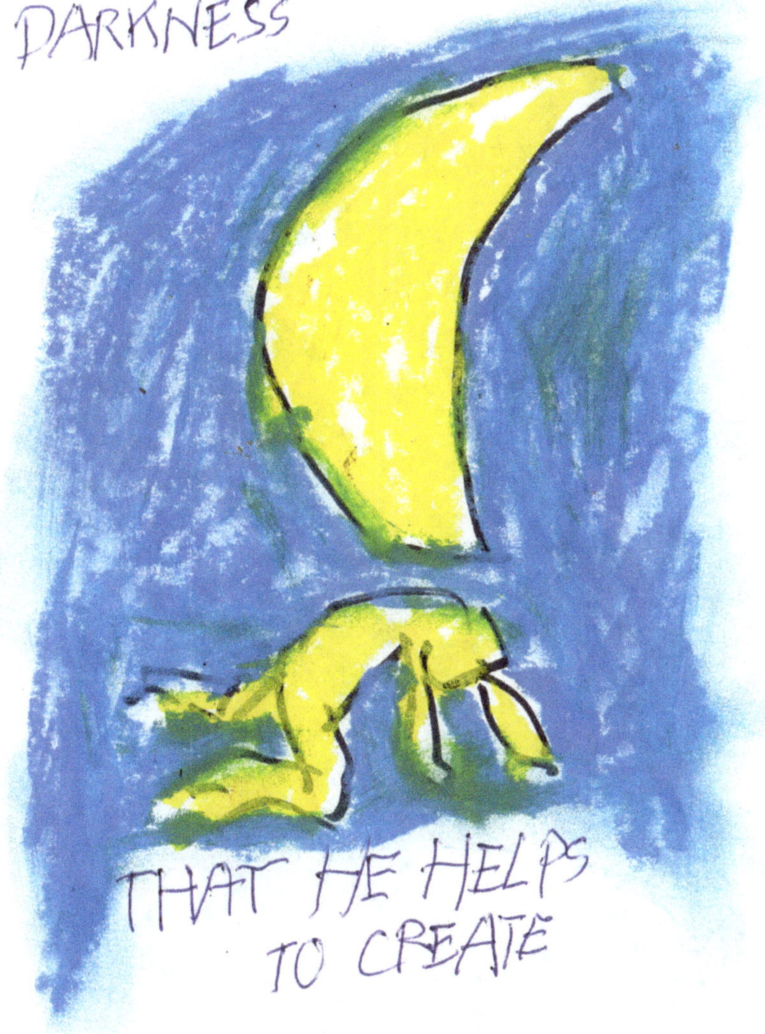

THE MOON SHINES
ONLY FOR THE EXTREMES OF
DARKNESS
THAT HE HELPS
TO CREATE

THE COMETS

ARE TORCHES LIT BY THE UNIVERSE PROCLAIMING TENTATIVE CONTINUATION

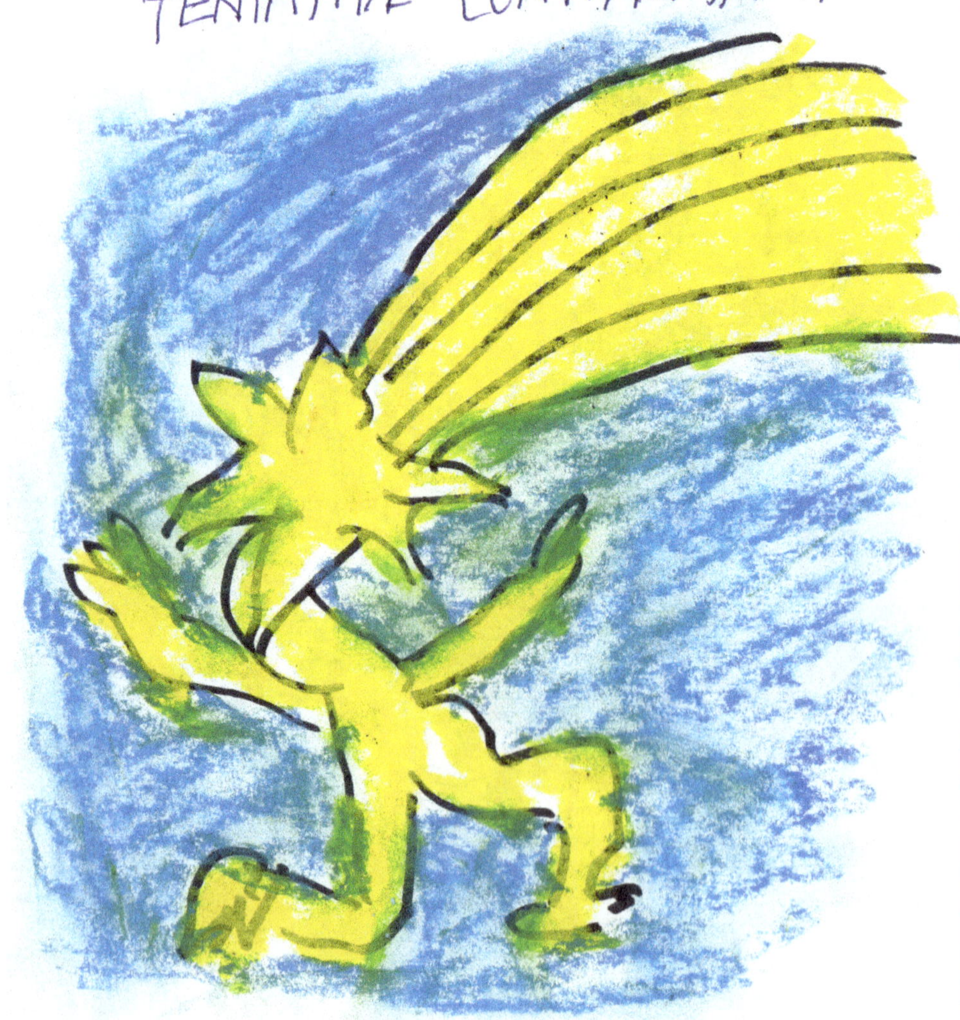

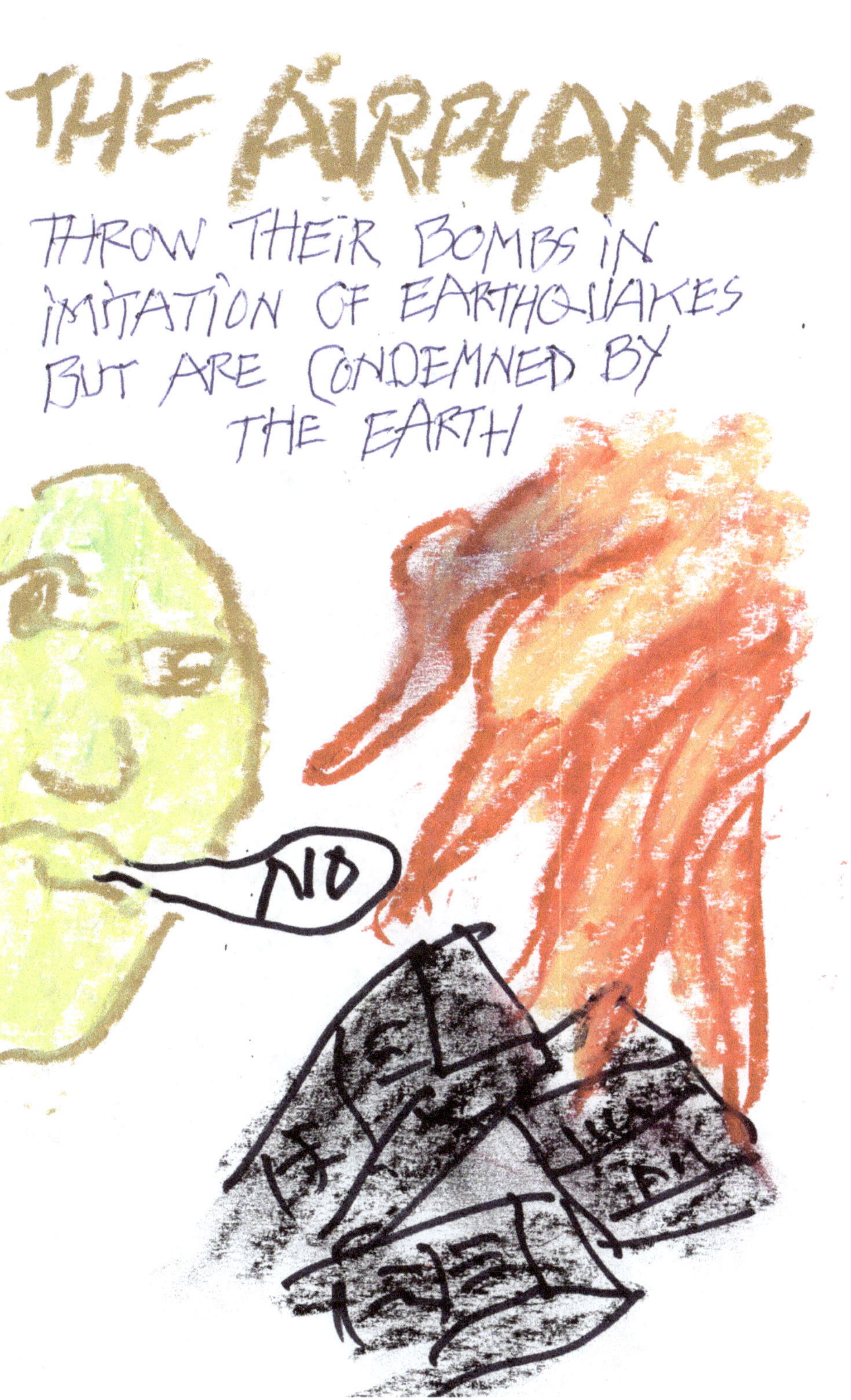

THE AIRPLANES
THROW THEIR BOMBS IN
IMITATION OF EARTHQUAKES
BUT ARE CONDEMNED BY
THE EARTH
NO

THE TARGETED

BABIES + THEIR MOMS
ABHORE THE SKY FOR ITS
CRUELTY

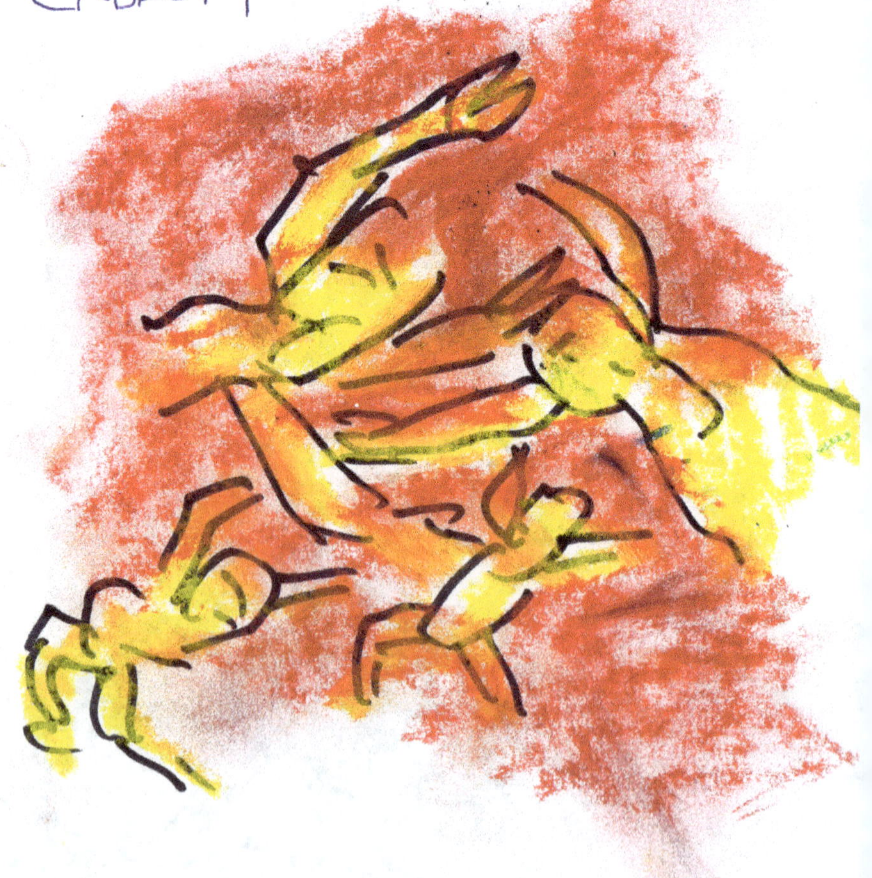

THE FOREVERSKY

DOES NOT PERMIT THE HUMANITY—
INFESTED SKY + ASSIGNS IT
TO HELL

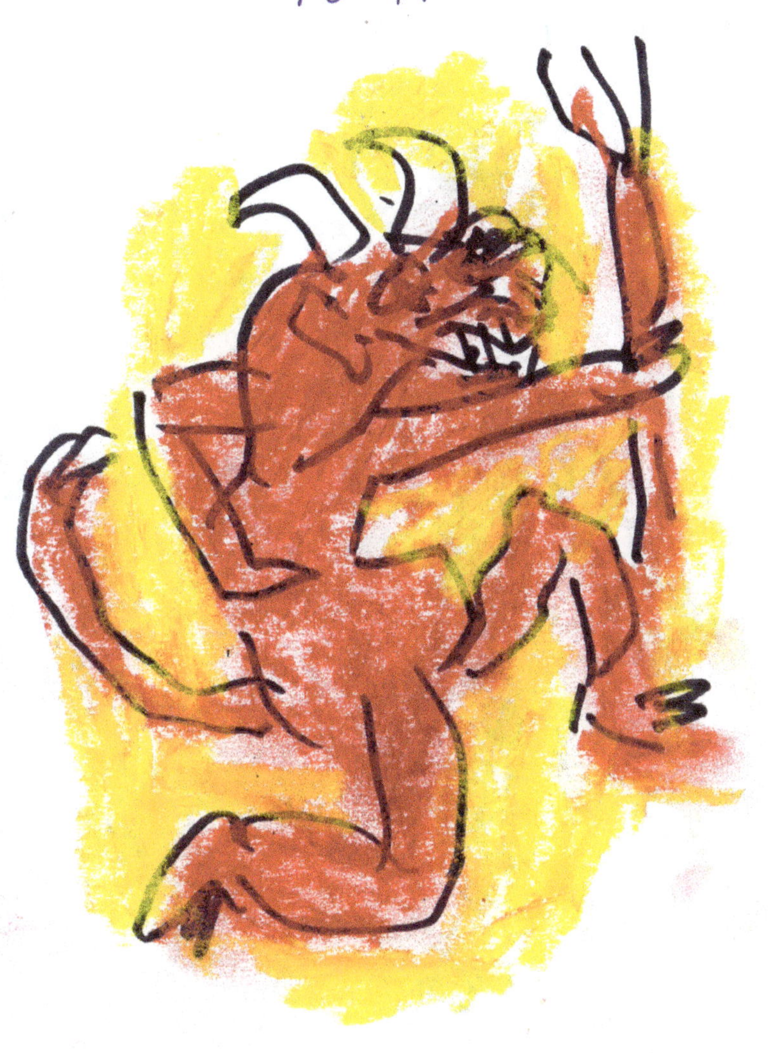

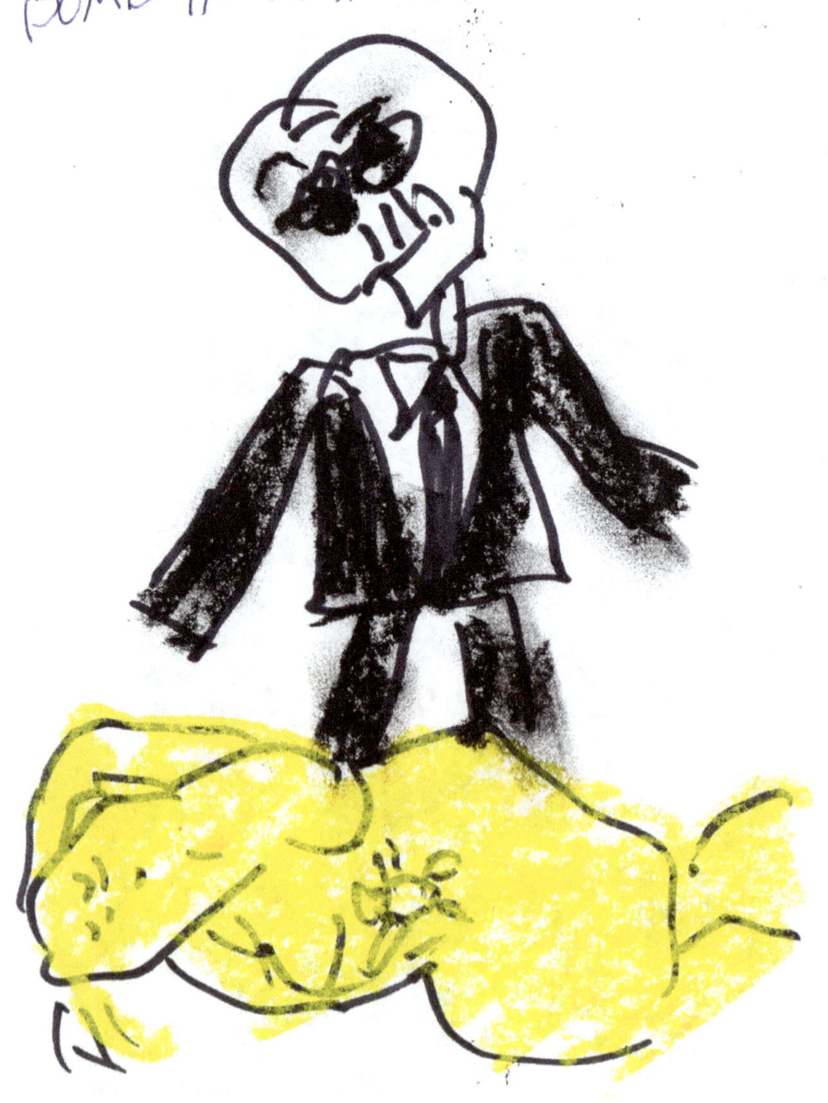

HELL 'ITSELF is
THE ADMINISTRATIONS EVIL AS
REPRESENTED BY A HUMANITY THAT
HAS LOST ITS EXISTENCE + TRIES TO
BOMB ITS WAY BACK INTO IT

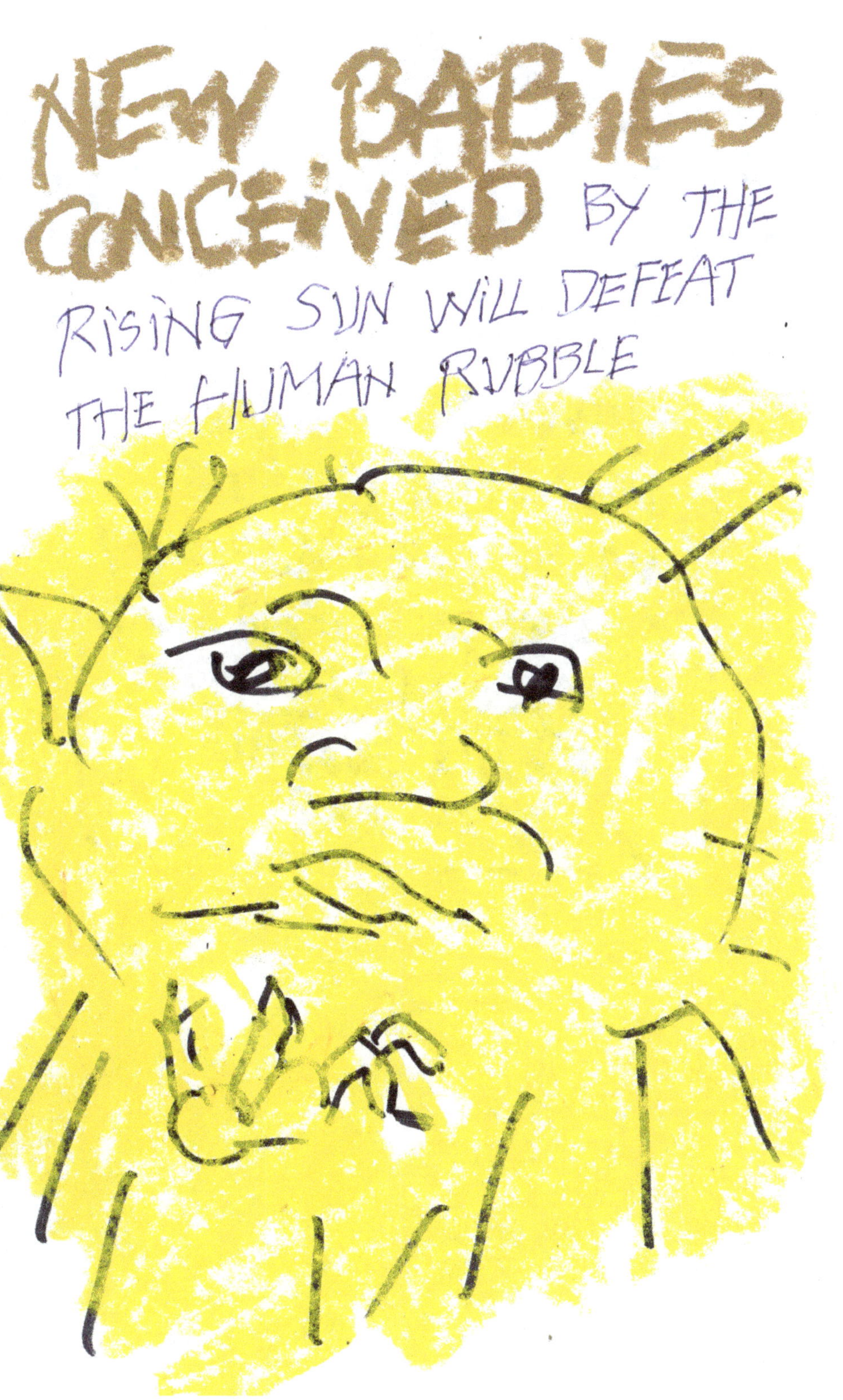

NEW BABIES
CONCEIVED BY THE
RISING SUN WILL DEFEAT
THE HUMAN RUBBLE

WE
POSSIBILITARIANS

HUMANS, BECOME
ESSENTIAL BECAUSE
WHEN TIME PASSES AWAY
CHANCE WILL BE NO MORE
ONLY ESSENCE WILL PREVAIL
ANGELUS SILESIUS
30 YEARS WAR

AND WE
WHO LEARNED FROM COVID
THAT WE ARE NOT ESSENTIAL,
A DISTINCTION WHICH IS RESERVED
FOR DOCTORS NURSES SUPERMARKETS.
+ GASSTATIONS

AND MUST THEREFORE

LEARN OUR NON-ESSENTIALISM
AS A SERIOUS MATTER THAT DEFIES
THE PREVAILING LOGIC

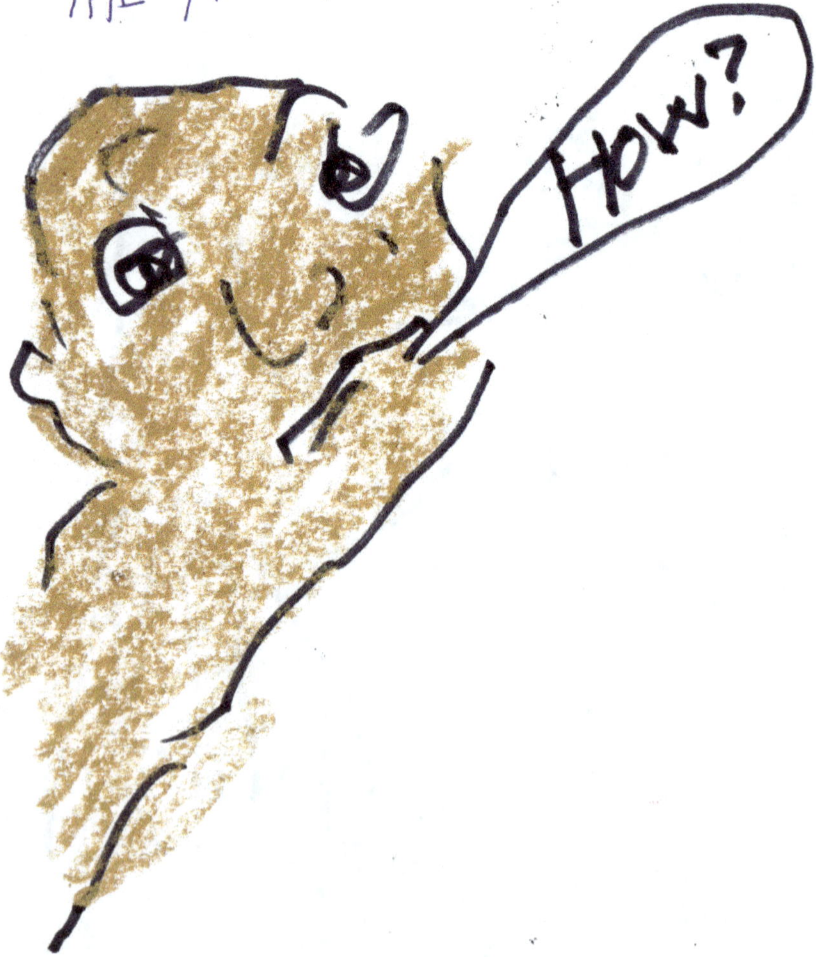

WITH HELP FROM ANGELUS SILESIUS

WHO SAID: THE ROSE HAS NO WHY, IT BLOSSOMS BECAUSE IT BLOSSOMS + HAS BLOSSOMED SO FOR ETERNITY

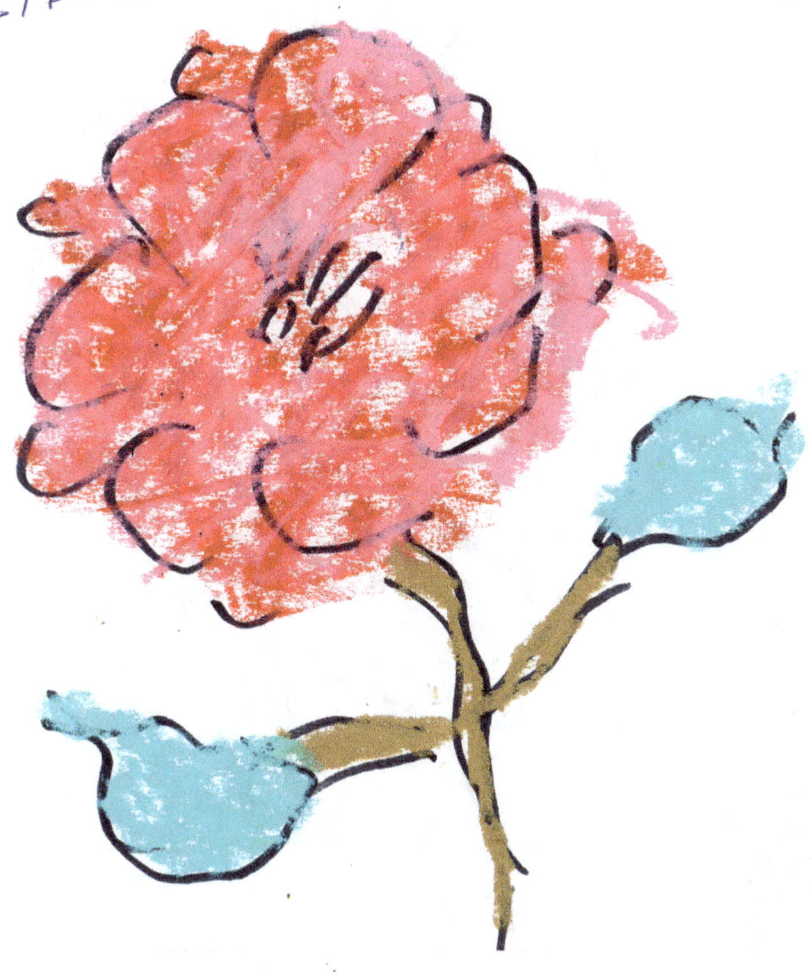

BUT WE NOT PRIVILEGED TO BE ROSES CAN NEVERTHELESS TAKE COMFORT IN THE ROSE'S INEXPLICABLE SENSE-MAKING

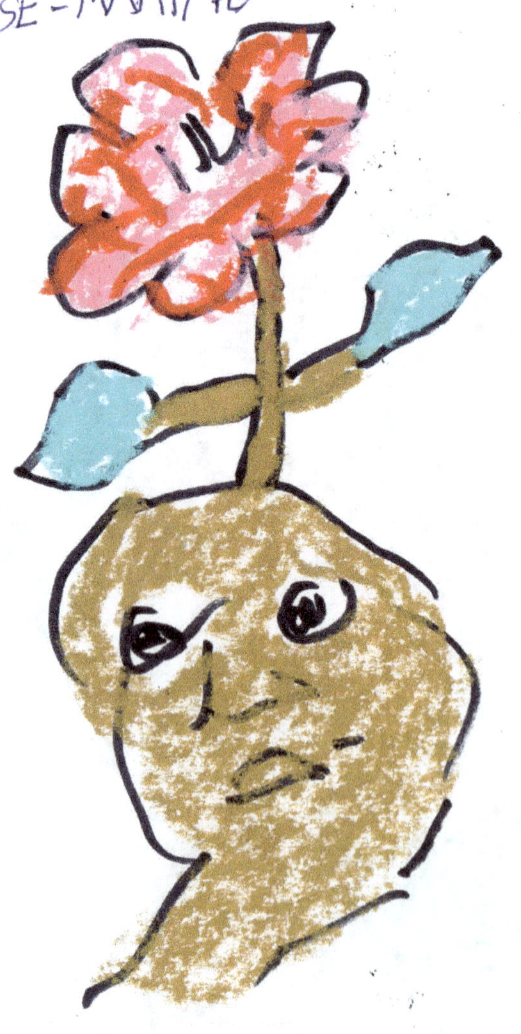

WHICH POINTS

TO THE FACT THAT EXACTLY OUR
NON-ESSENTIALISM IS URGENTLY
NEEDED AS WESTERN CIVILIZATIONS
SENSE COLLAPSES UNDERNEATH
BOMBED HOSPITALS

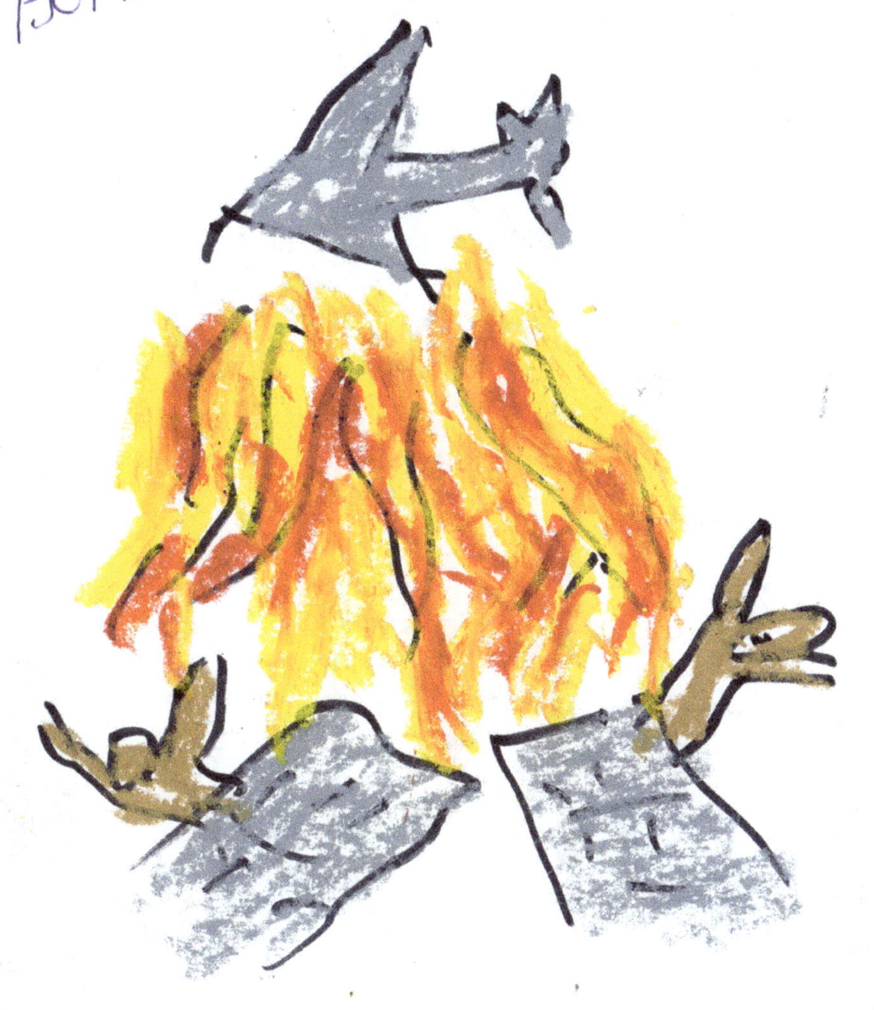

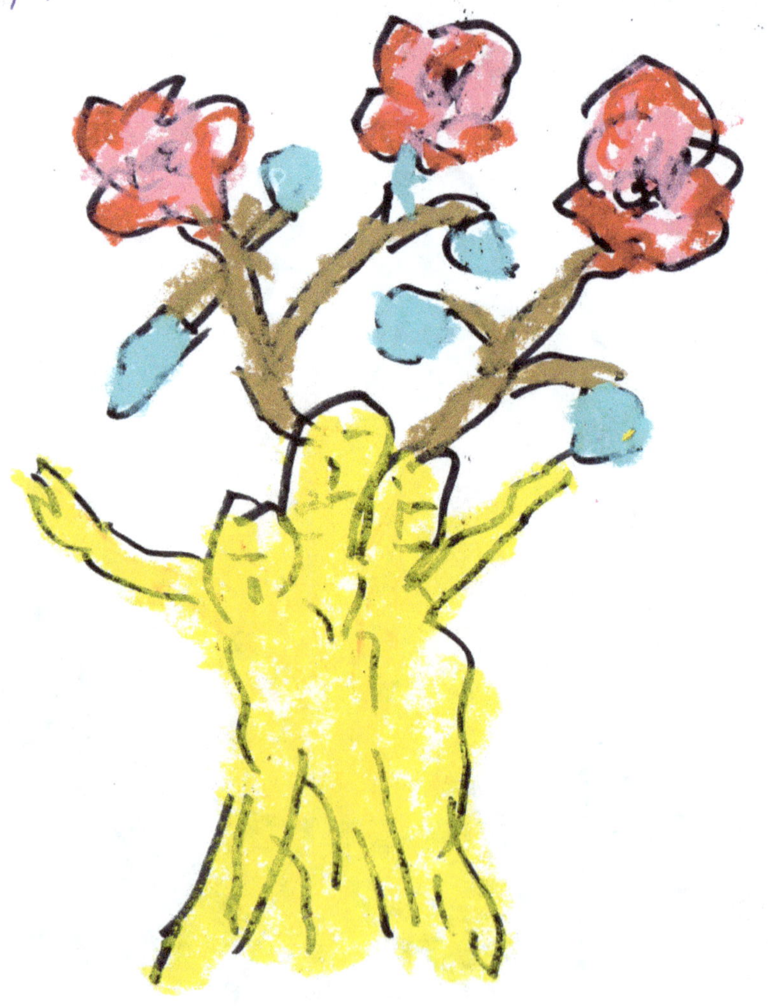
+ BOTH SENSE
+ REALITY
HAVE TO BE RE-INVENTED

WE
POSSIBILITARIANS

LîFE+DEATH

SîMULTANEOUSLY

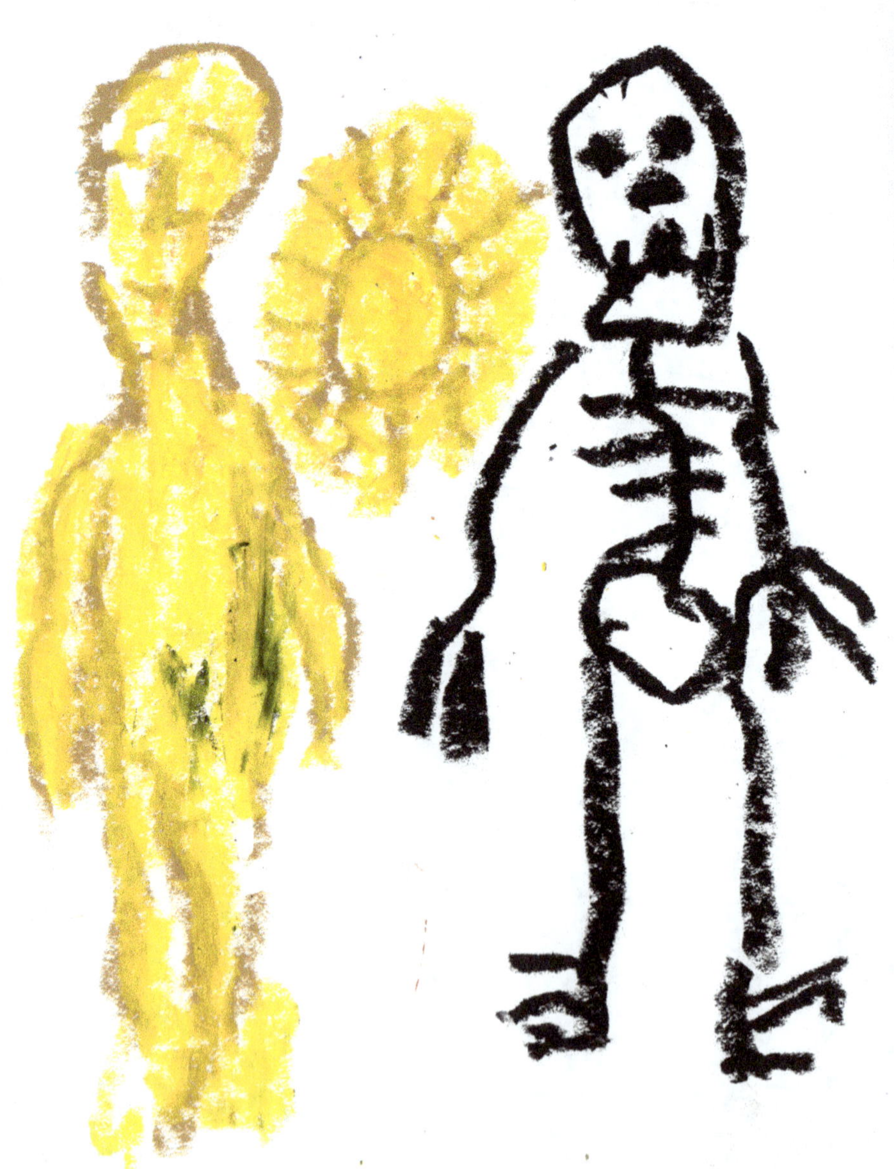

READY/ UNREADY

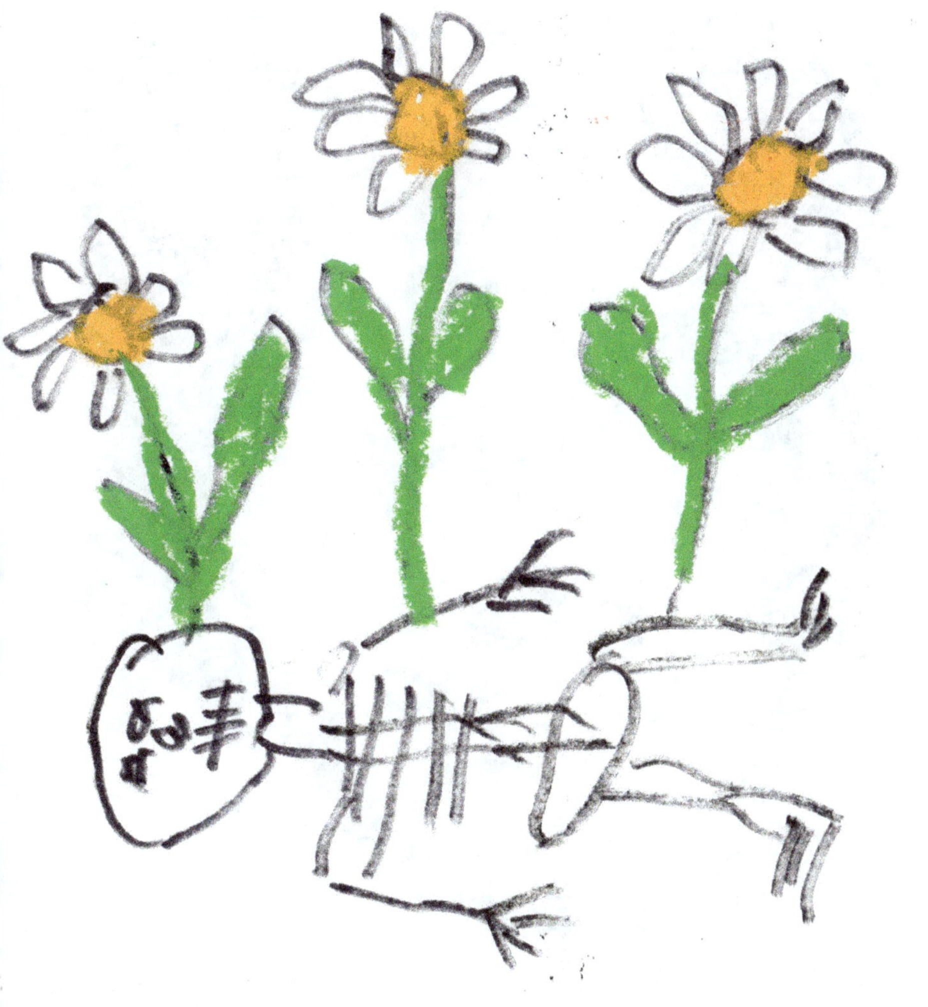

REPRESENTED

BY LIFE'S UNREADY INSTITUTIONS

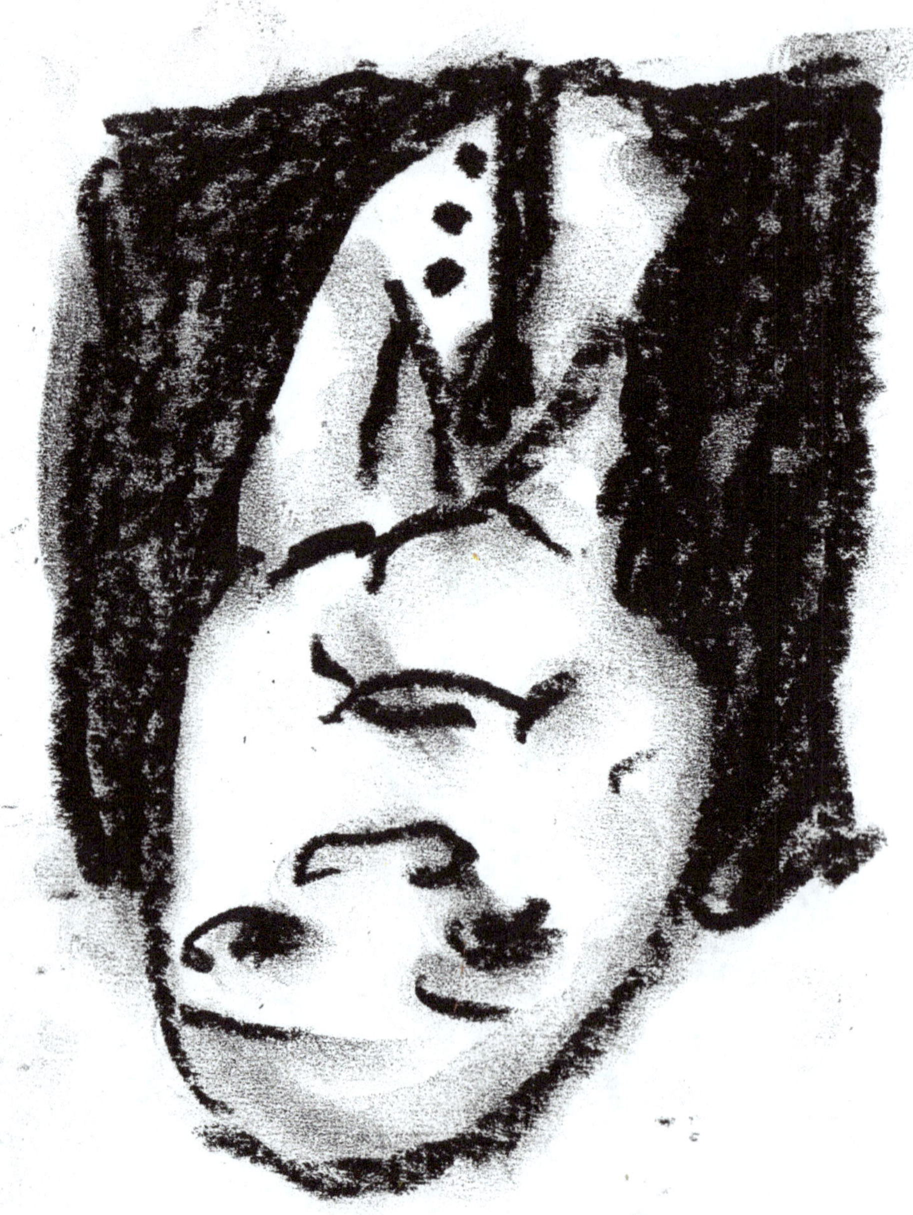

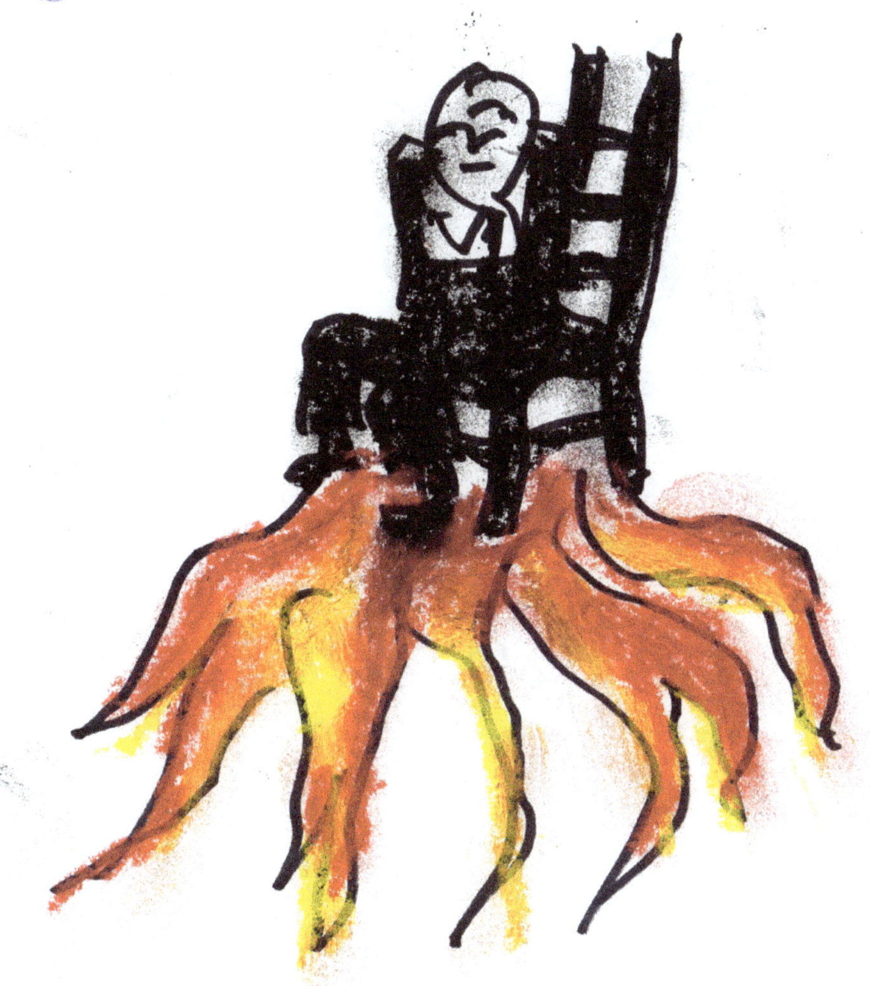

GIVEN TO DEATH
BY LIFE'S BOMBARDERS

WHO CLAIM TO
PURSUE LIFE WITH THEIR
INDISCRIMINATE DEATHS

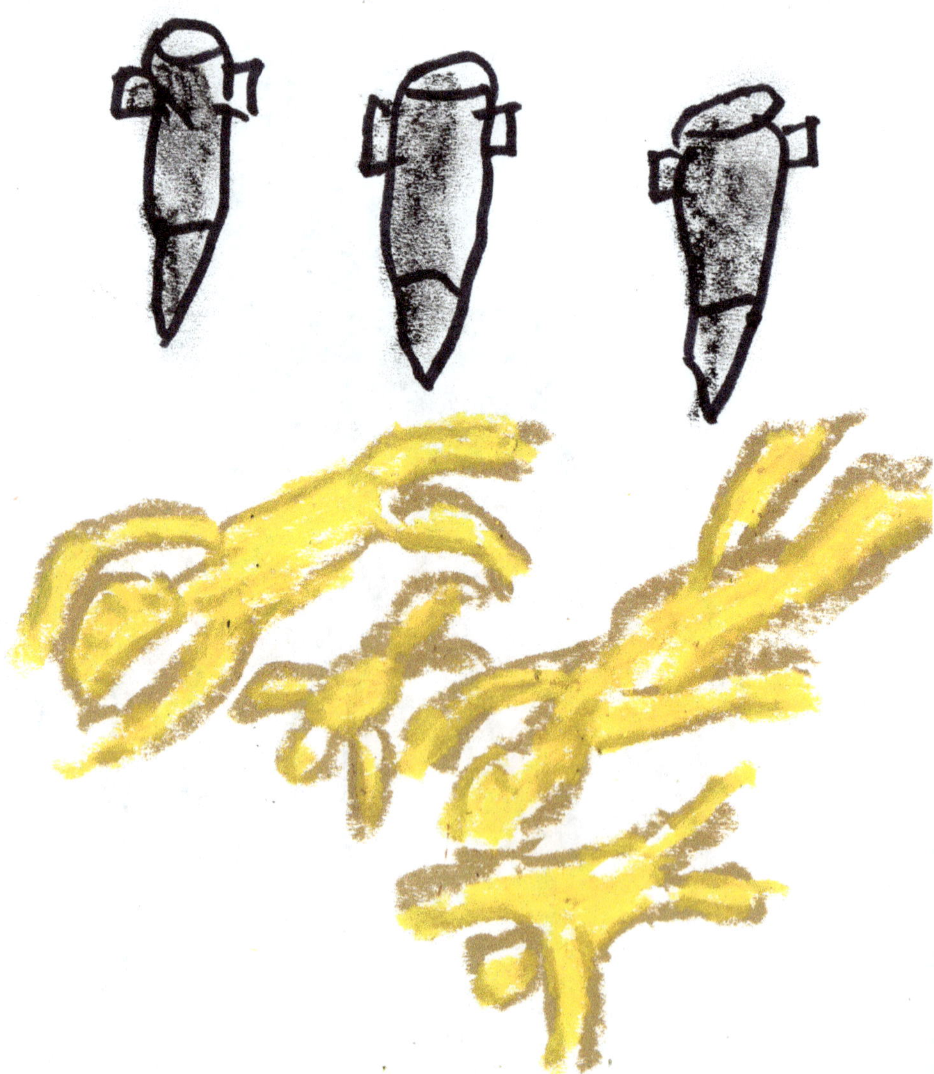

PURSUE LIFE WITH THEIR

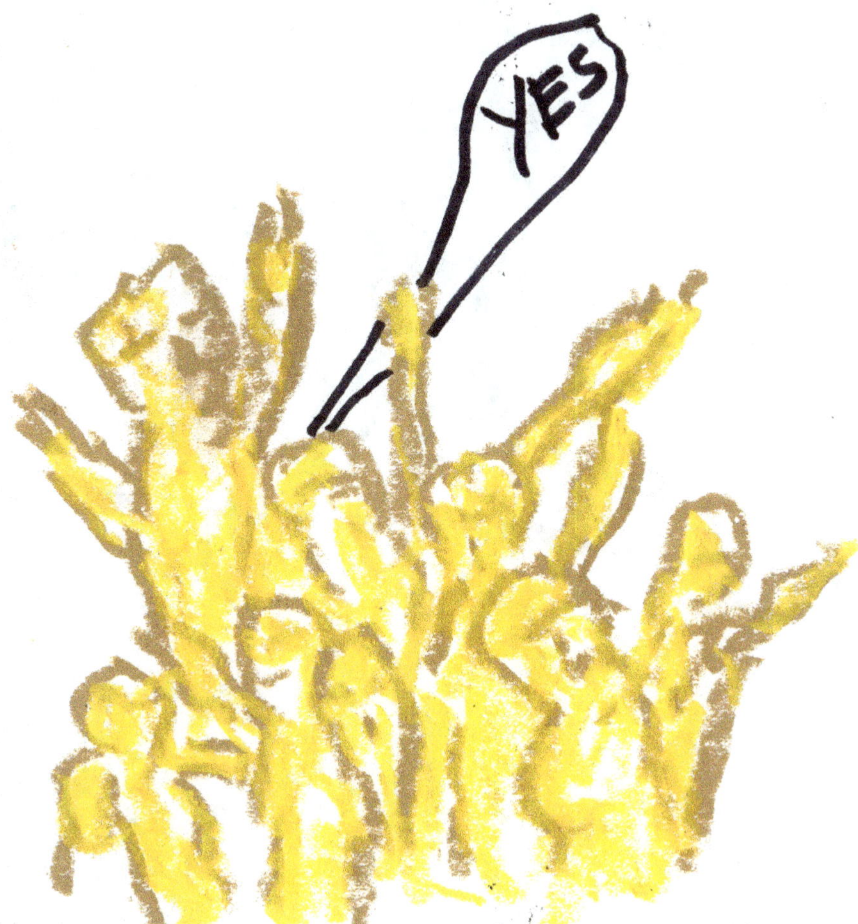
+YET WE
MUST BE OBLIGED
BY OUR READYNESS
+ MUST
YES
+YET WE MUST BE

You
possibilitarians

WHERE is
your
possibilitarian
Land

YOU MUST BRIDLE YOUR LAZY HORSE

+DANCE to THE

DRUM OF POST-DESTRUCTION

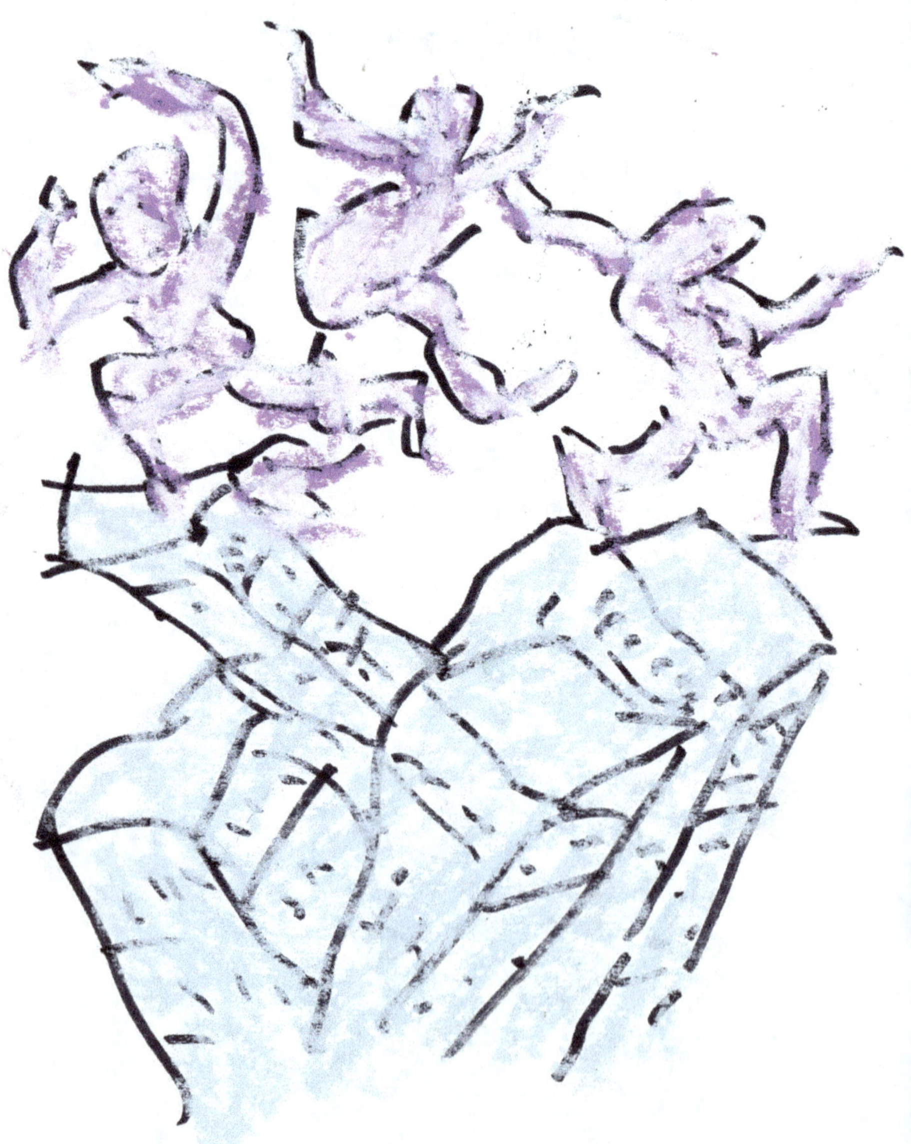

AND THE DING DONG OF THE DEATH-LIFE MARCHERS

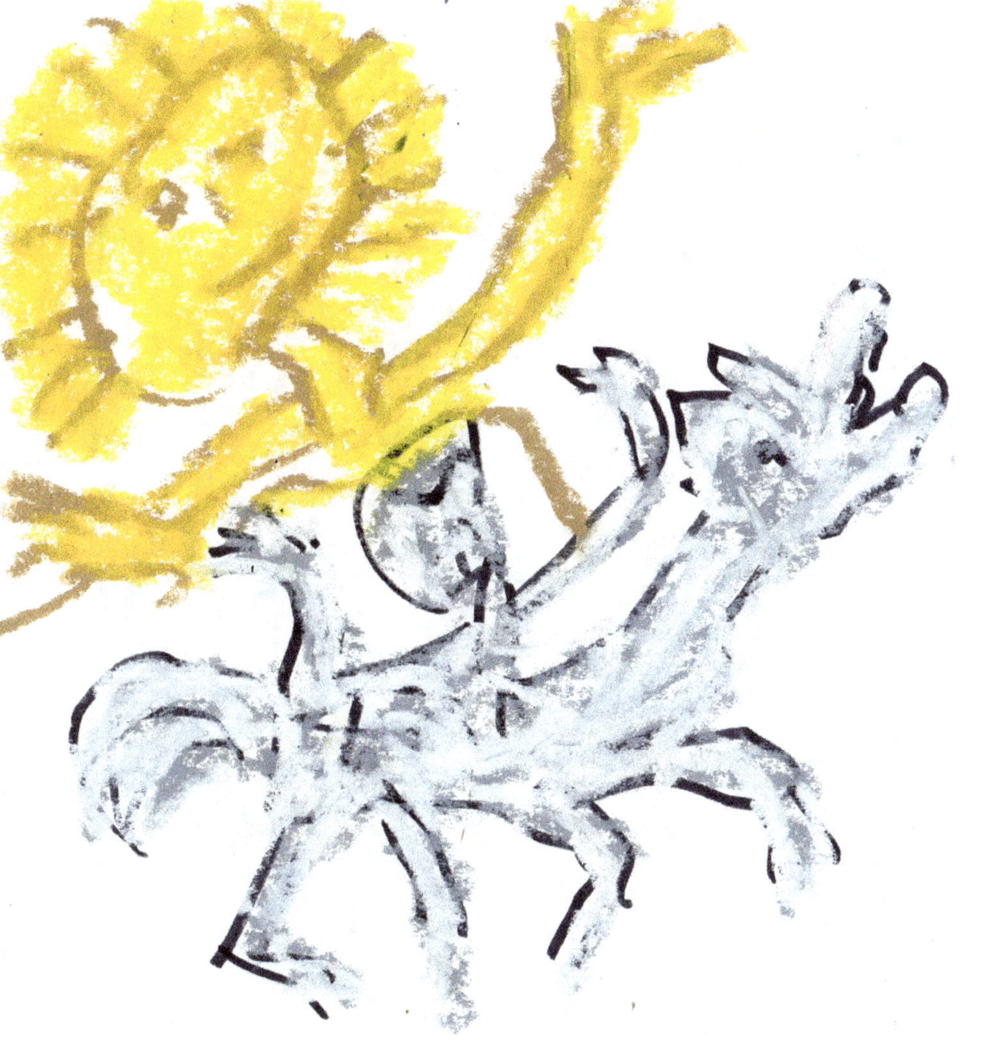

WITH THEIR
BATTLE-TORN FLAGS

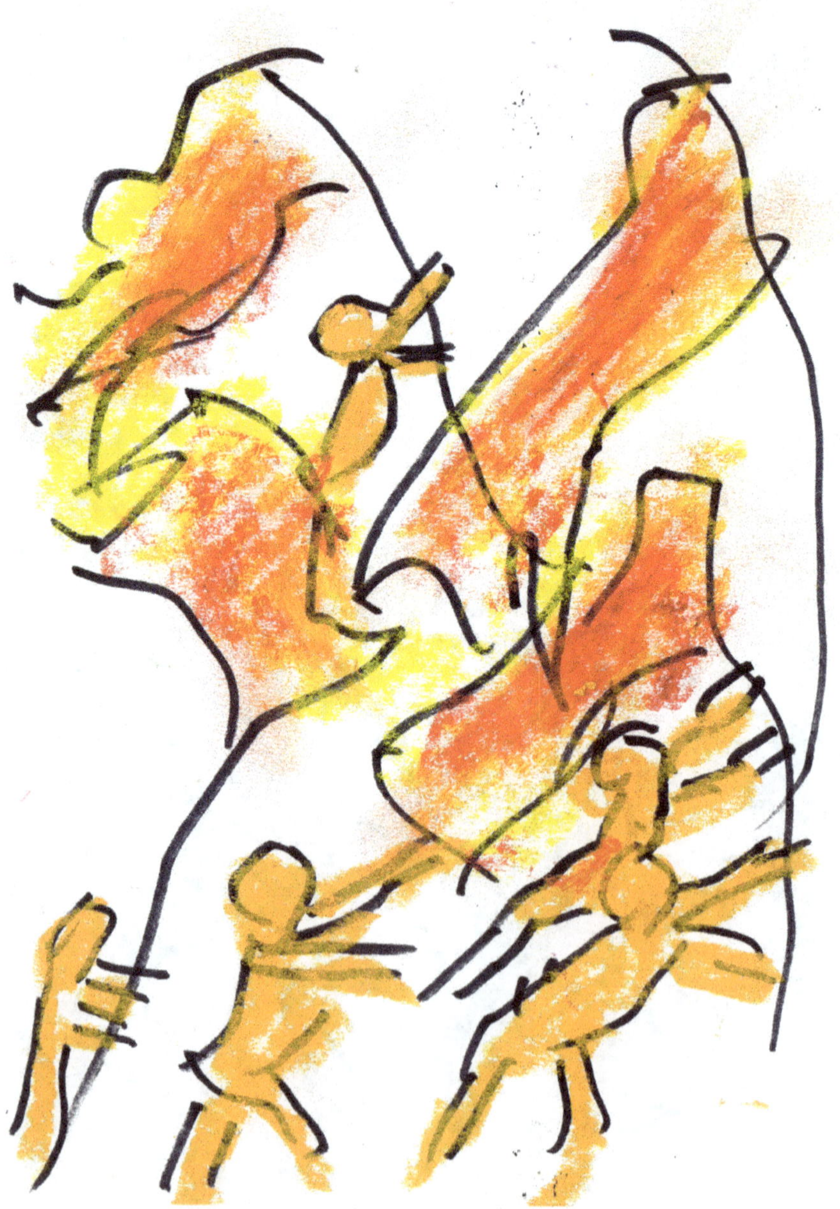

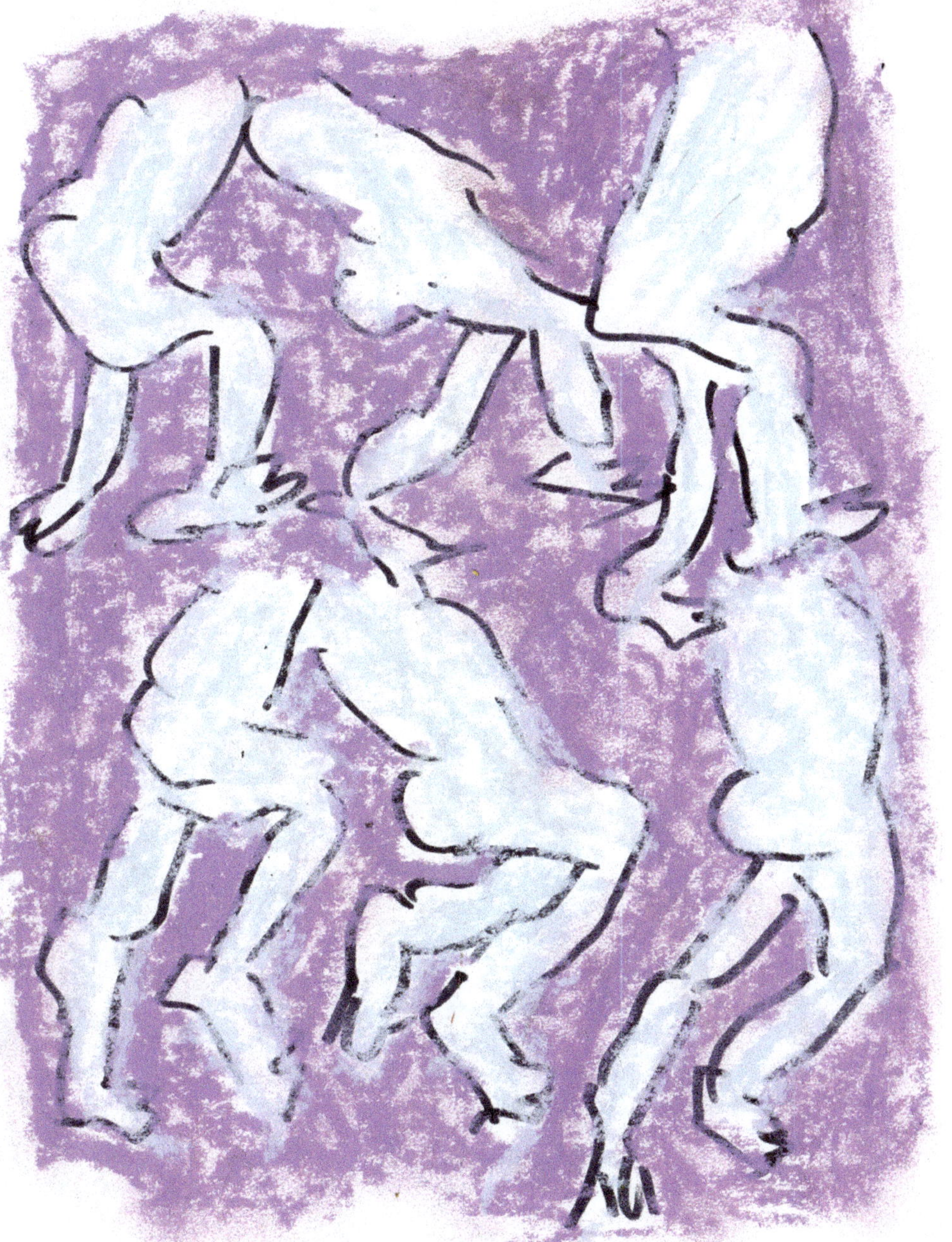
+DANCE THE
EVERYWHERE DANCE

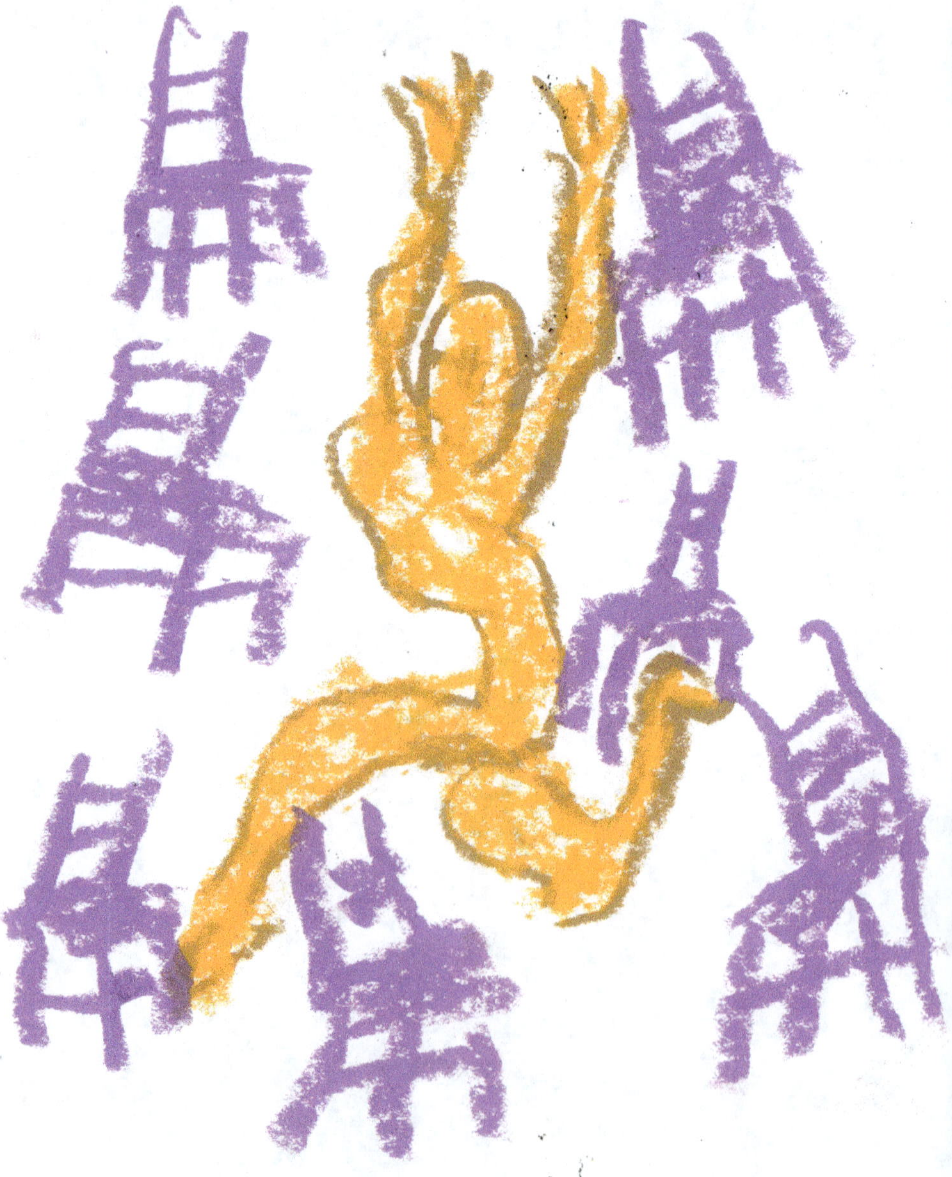
IN THE FACE OF
EVERYTHING

†IF YOU ARE NOT AVAILABLE

FOR WHATEVER SECONDARY REASON

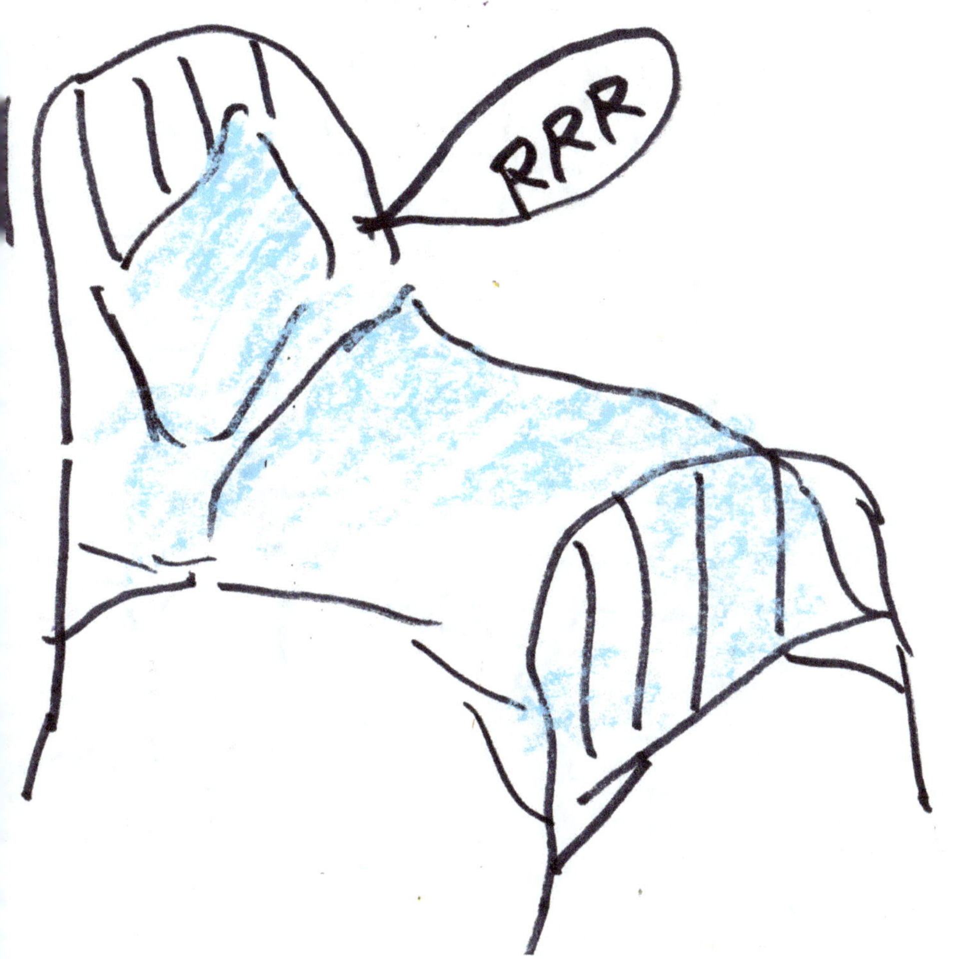

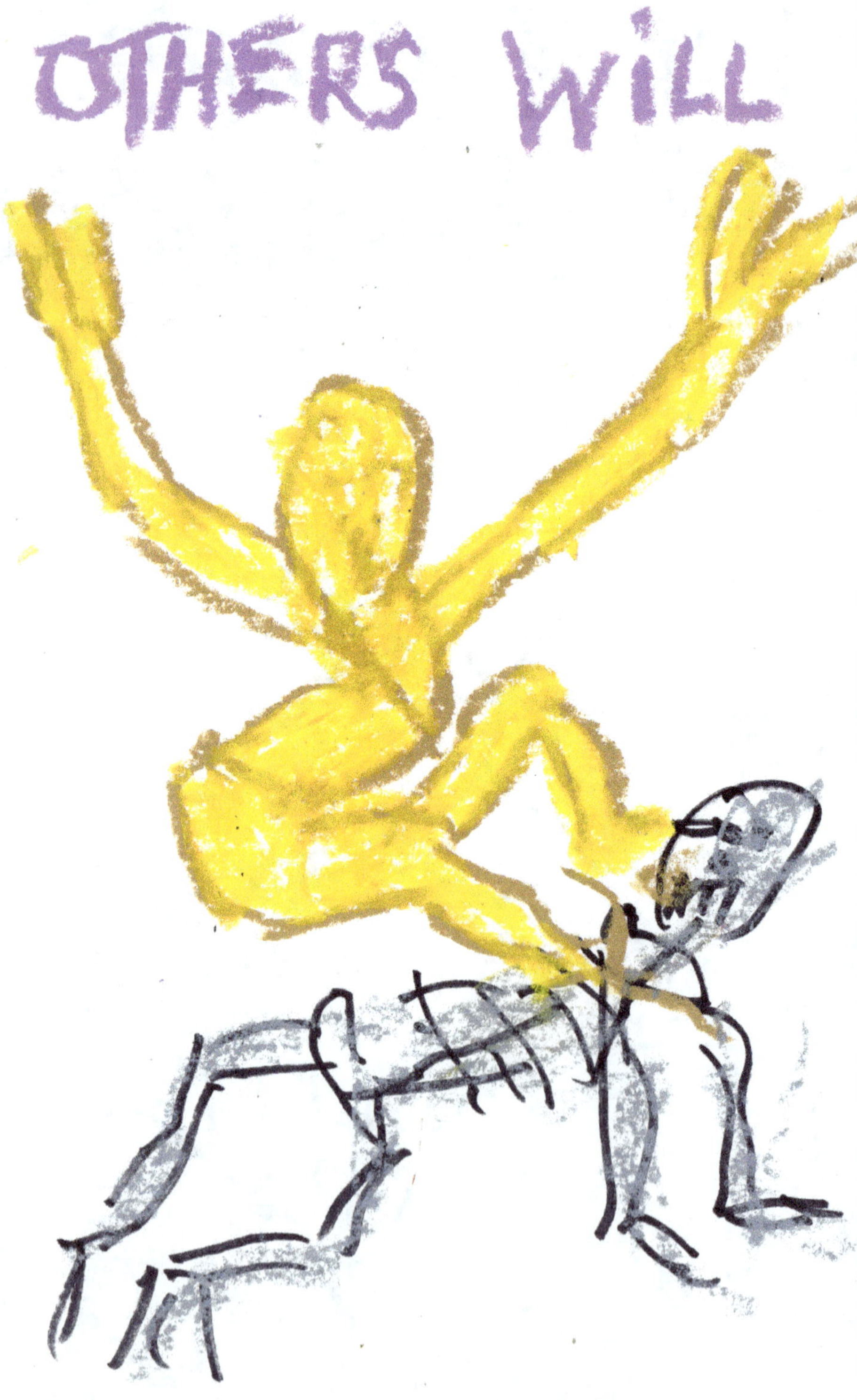

OTHERS WILL

OTHERS

+WiLL LiVE
YOUR SLoT of LiFE

+ PERFORM YOUR GLORIOUSLY

IRREPLACEABLE SKILL

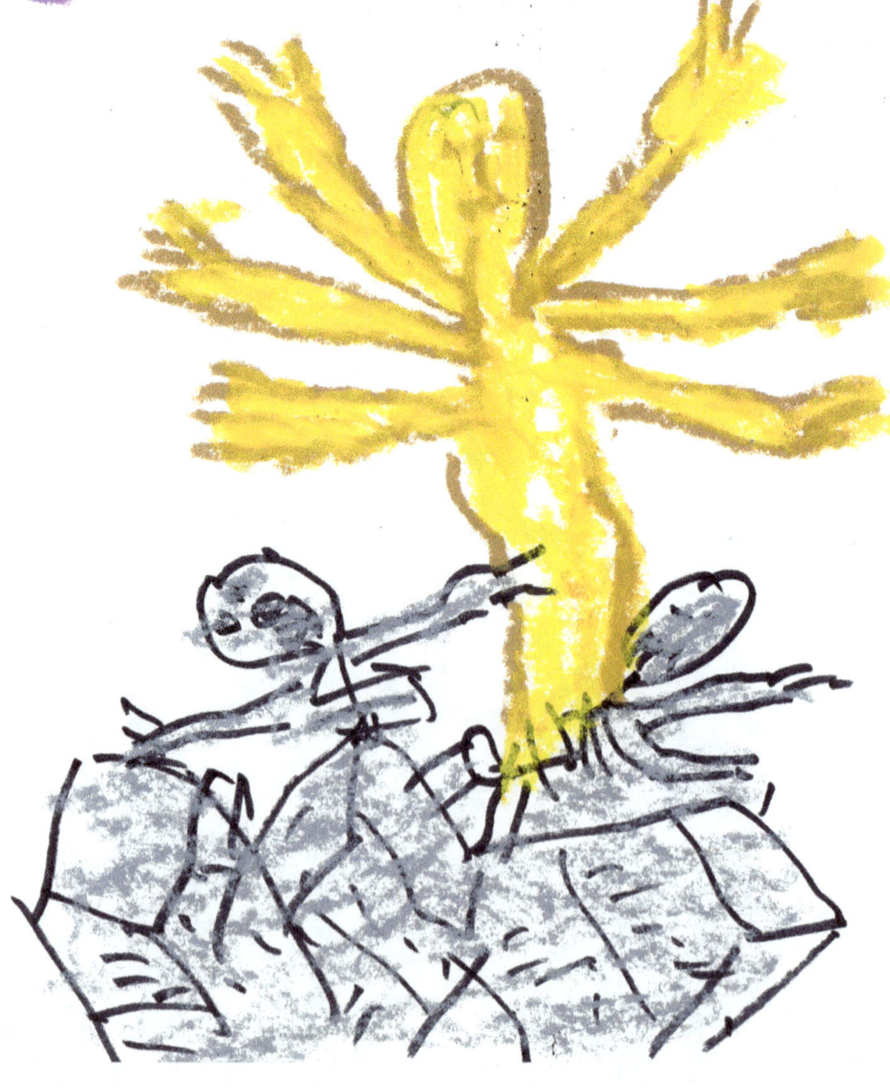

POSSIBILITARIAN

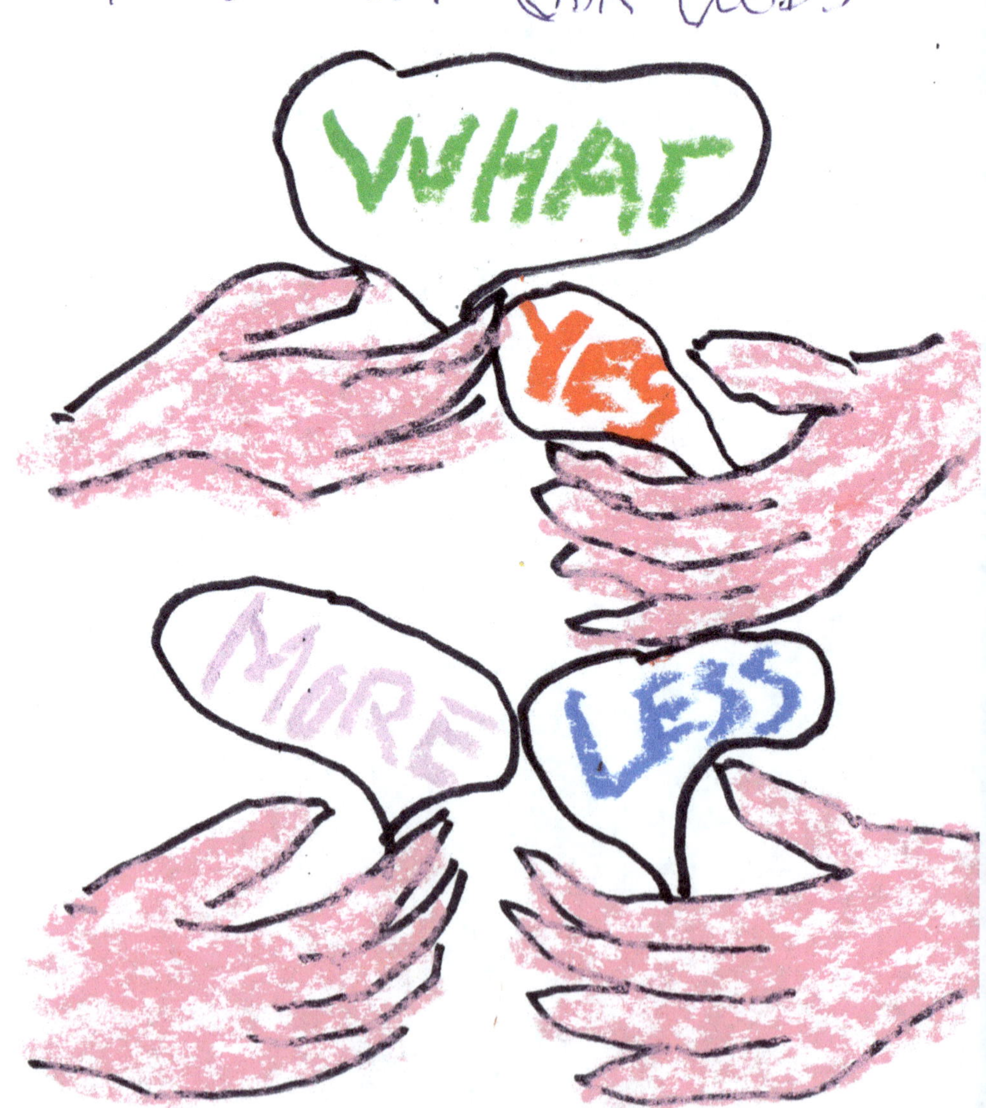

YOU LIFE HAVE
TO DELIVER YOUR GOODS
WHAT
YES
MORE
LESS

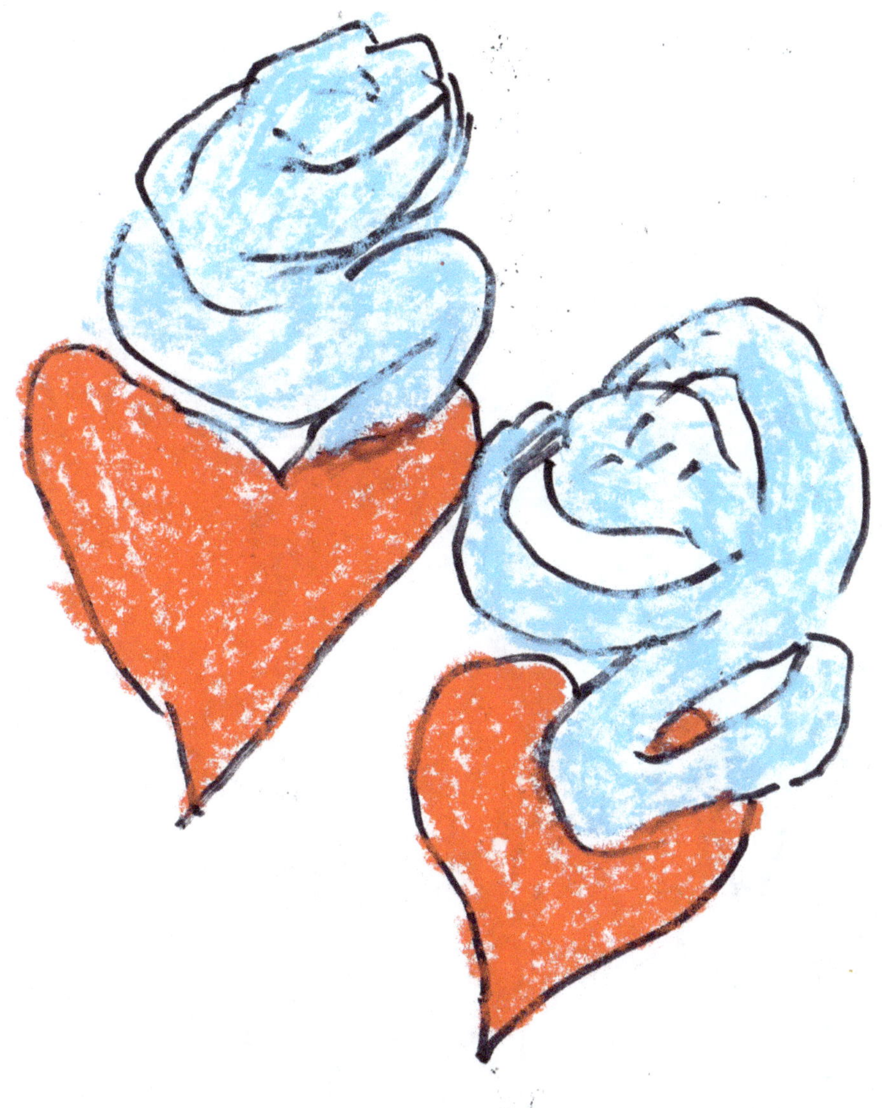
TO THE STARVING
SOULS

REGARDLESS
OF THE FLIMSY EXCUSES OF OVERFED CITIZENRIES

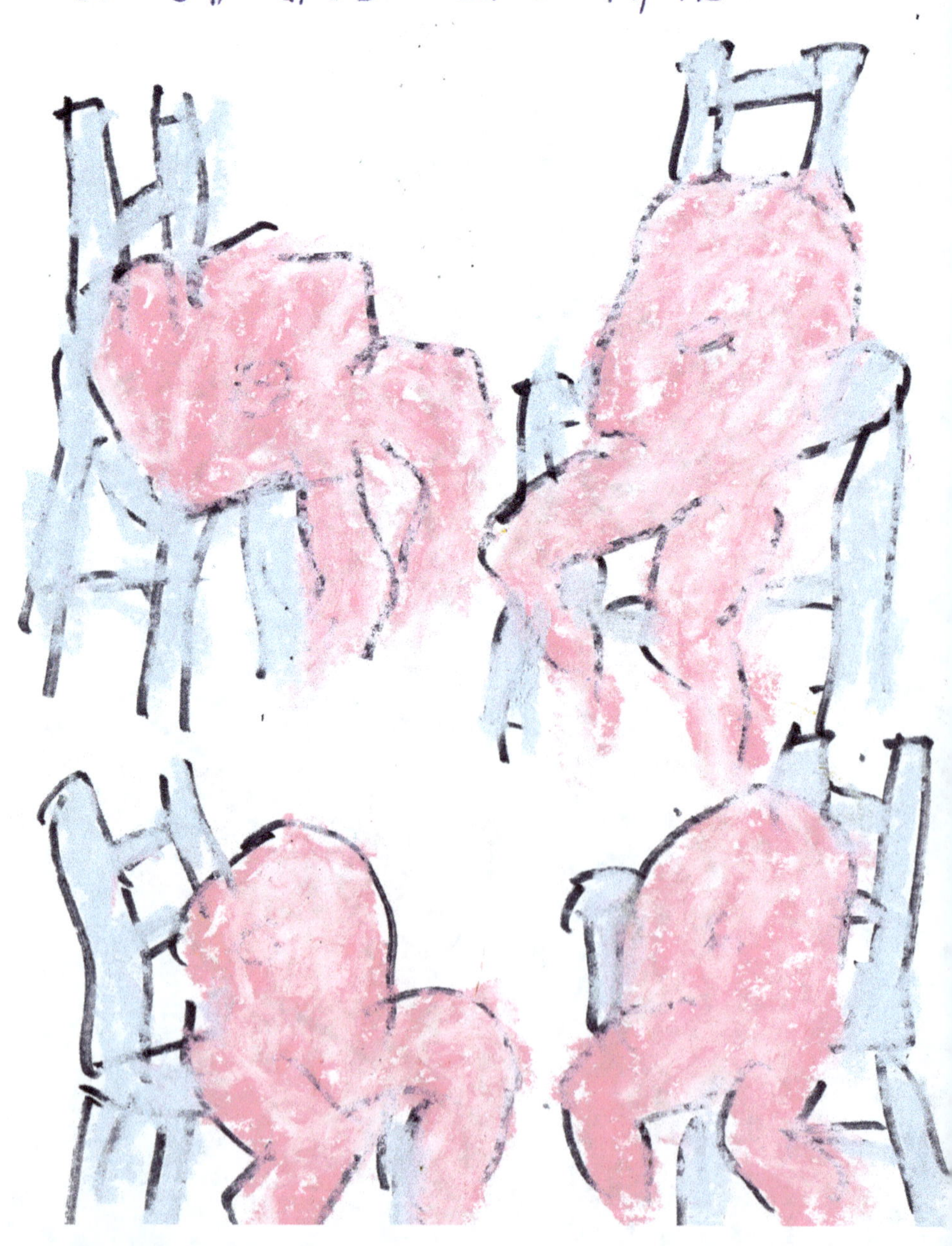

WHO DON'T REALIZE
THEIR STARVATION
WHO DON'T

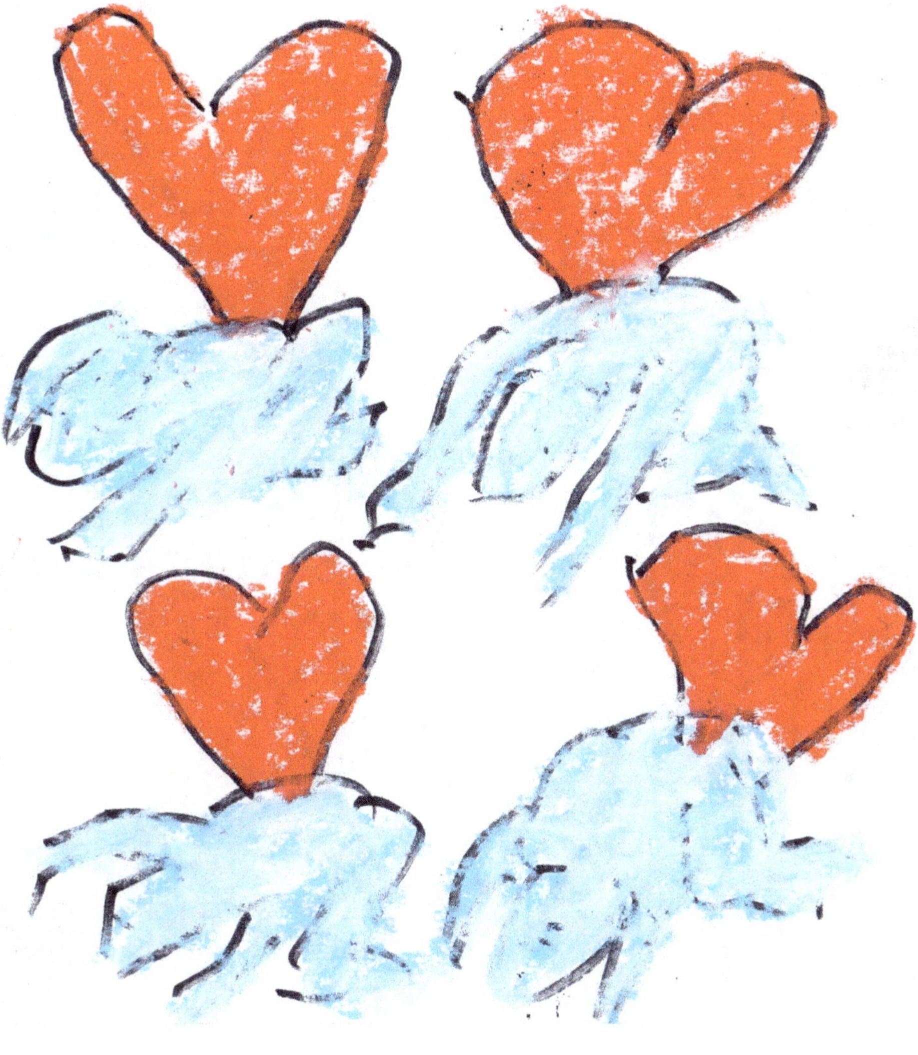

+LET THEM
CLIMB THE STEEP LADDERS TO
HEAVEN OR HELL

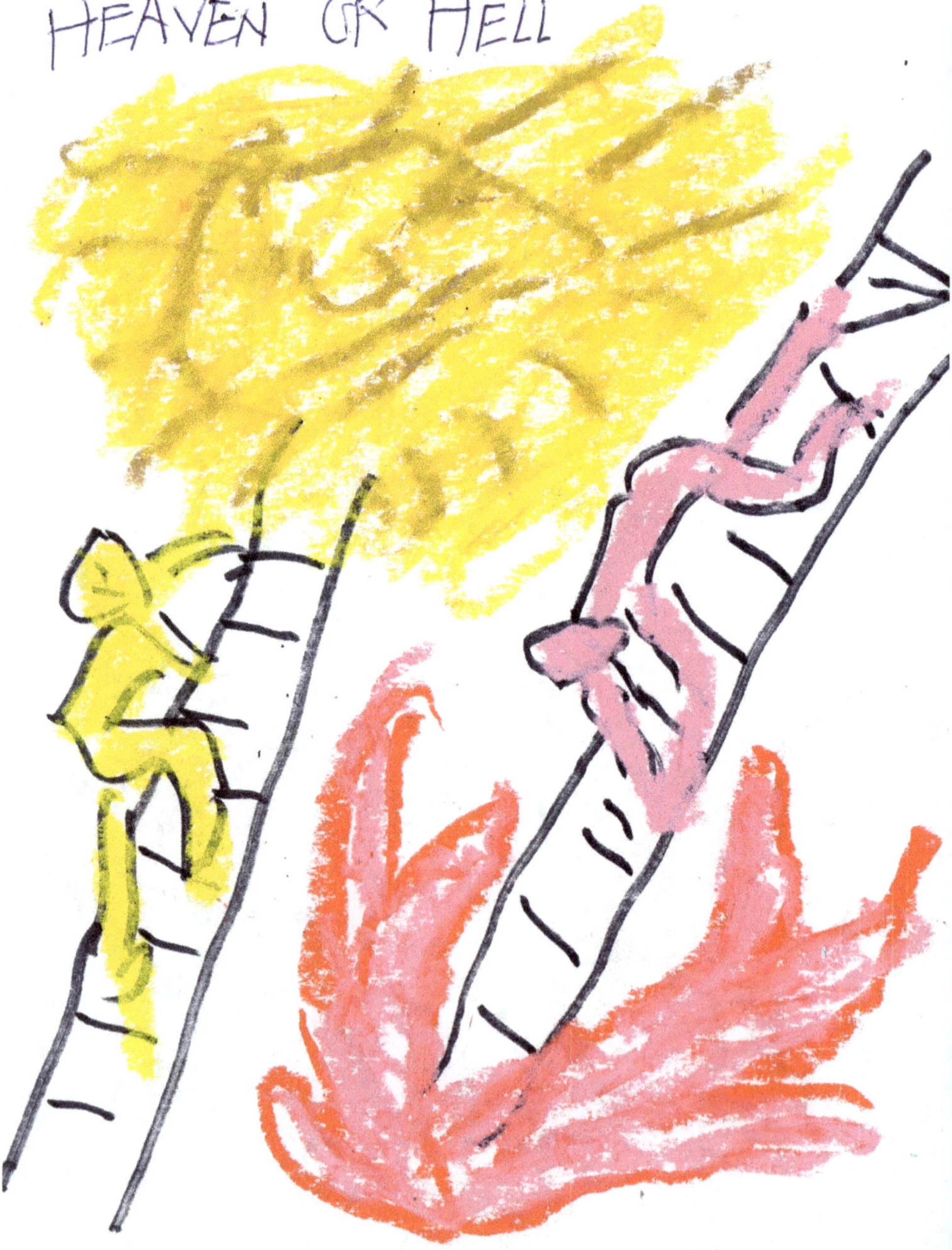

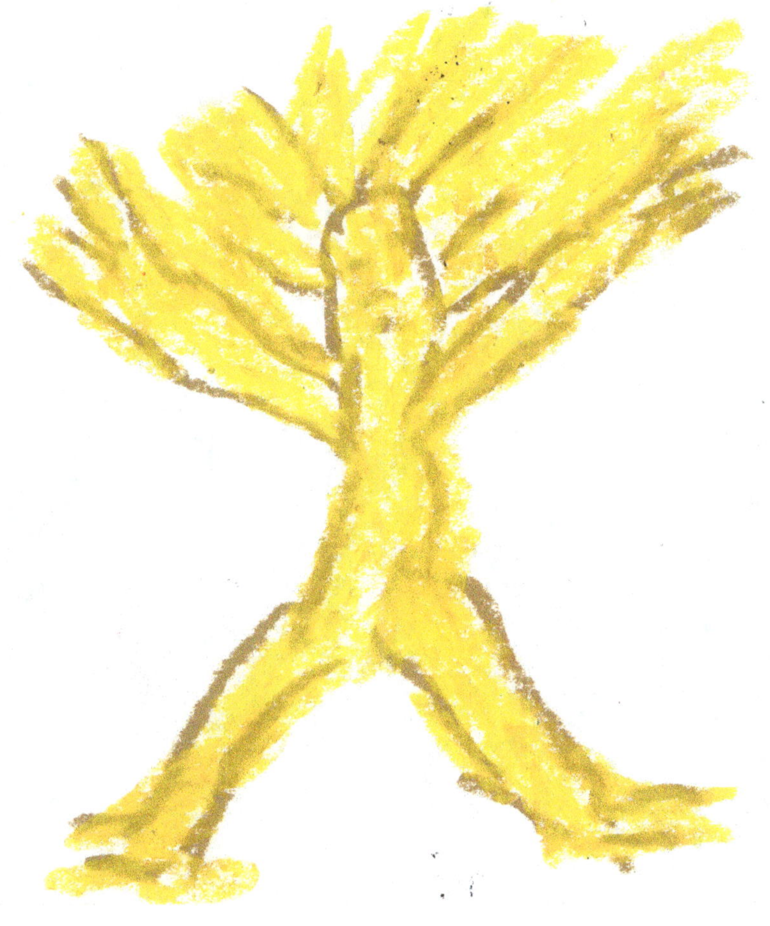

TO ACQUAINT THEM
WITH THE UNIVERSE'S
UNCOMPROMISING INTENTIONS, NAMELY
TO BE FORCED TO BE WHOLE

+ NOTHING LESS

ONLY THEN

CAN NORMALITY BE NORMAL
+ REALITY BE REAL

+THE 2 LEGGED

MONSTER WHO DEVOURS HOSPITALS +
SCHOOLS + REFUGEE CAMPS WILL BE
CAST OUT BY THE SAME TRUTH—
STARVED POPULATIONS OF THE EARTH

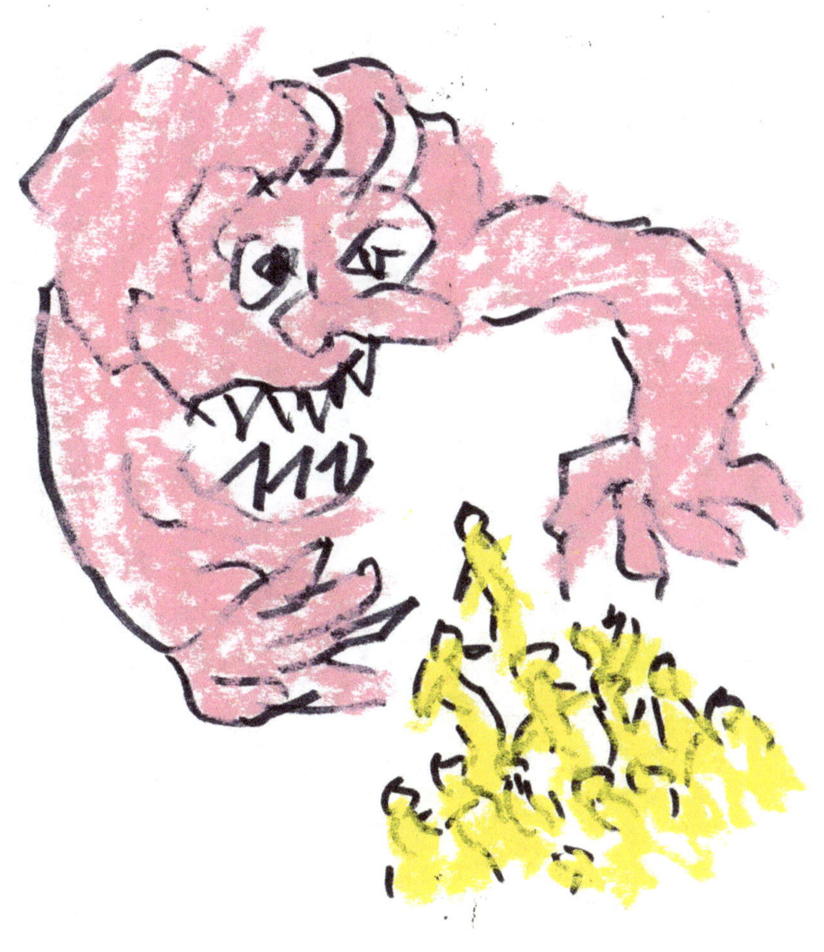

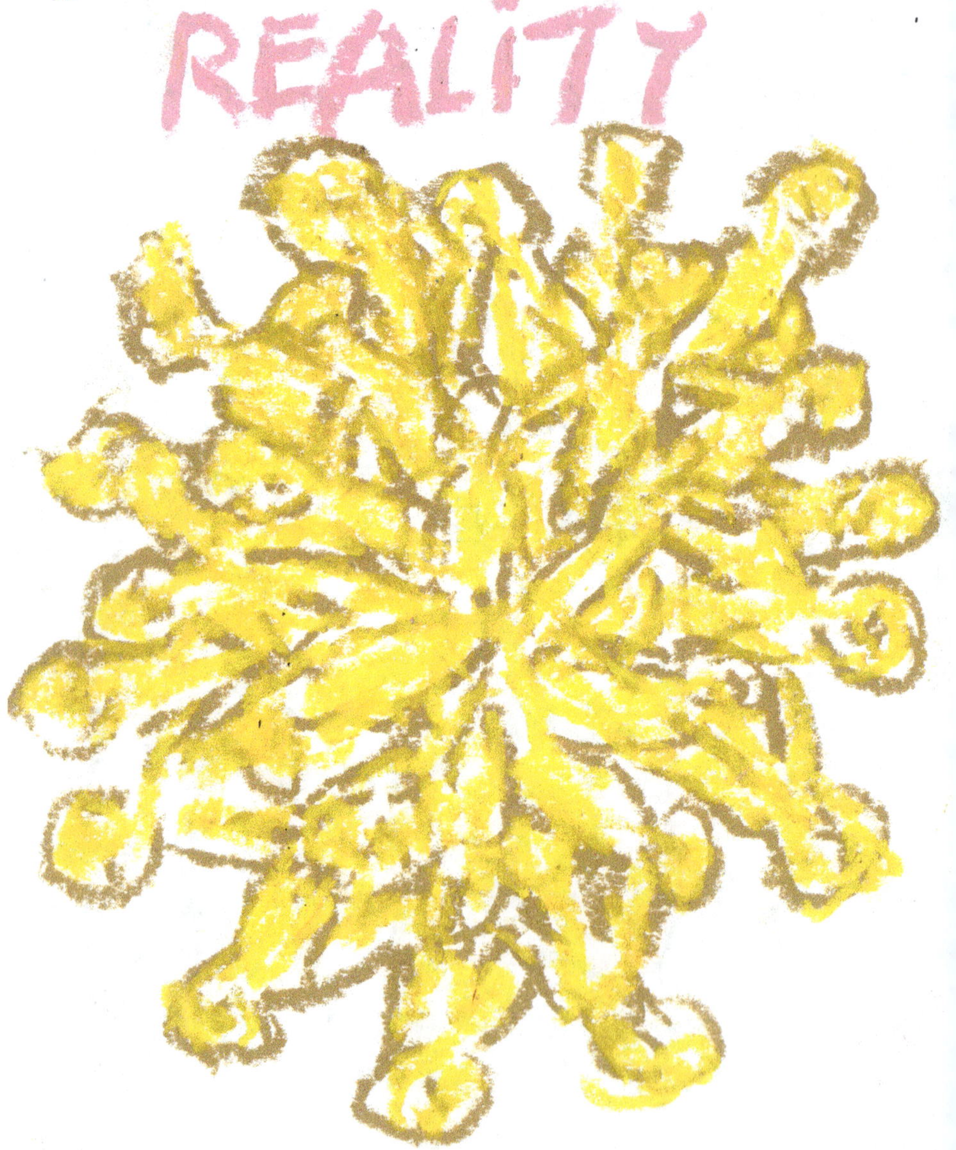

+ MADE TO MEET
ALL MOTHERS. BABIES FATHER
SISTERS BROTHERS IN THE REAL
REALITY

POSSIBILITARIANS

[INFLAMED]

BY THE EARTH'S FLAMES

WE WHO HAVE

BEEN INFLAMED BY THE EARTH'S FLAMES

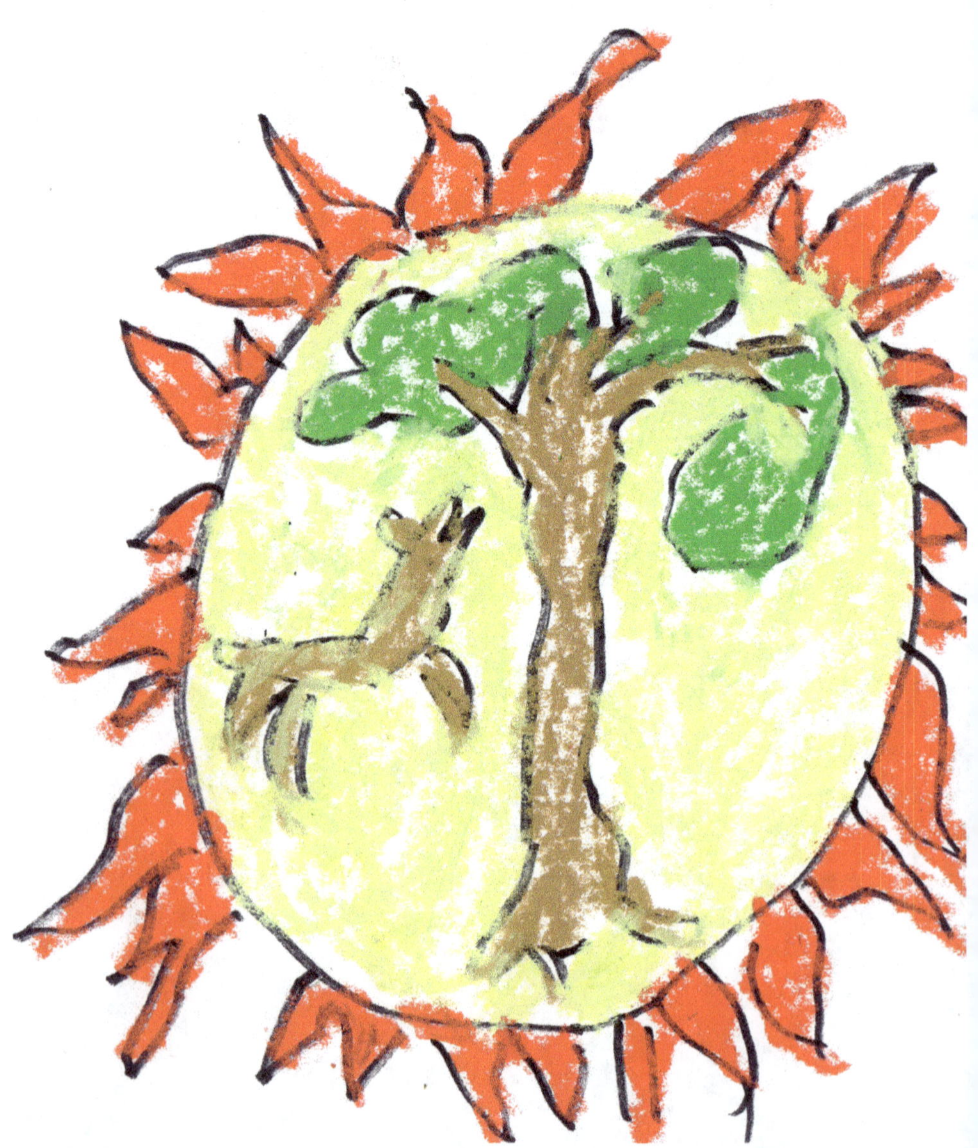

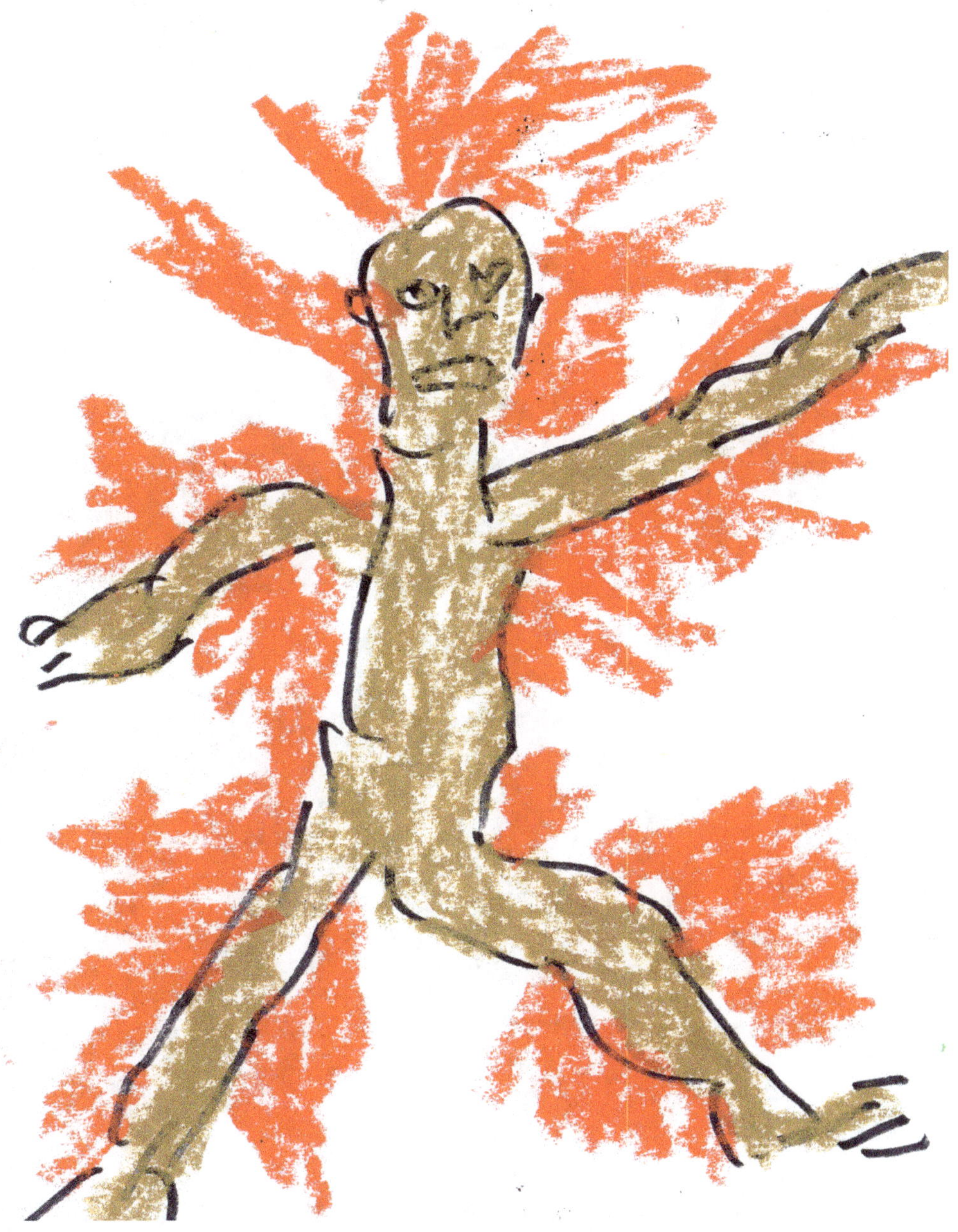
ARE NOW
INFLAMMATORY EARTHLINGS

+ THEREFORE

ALMOST READY TO COOL DOWN OUR INSATIABLE HUNGER FOR THE MORE OF EVERYTHING

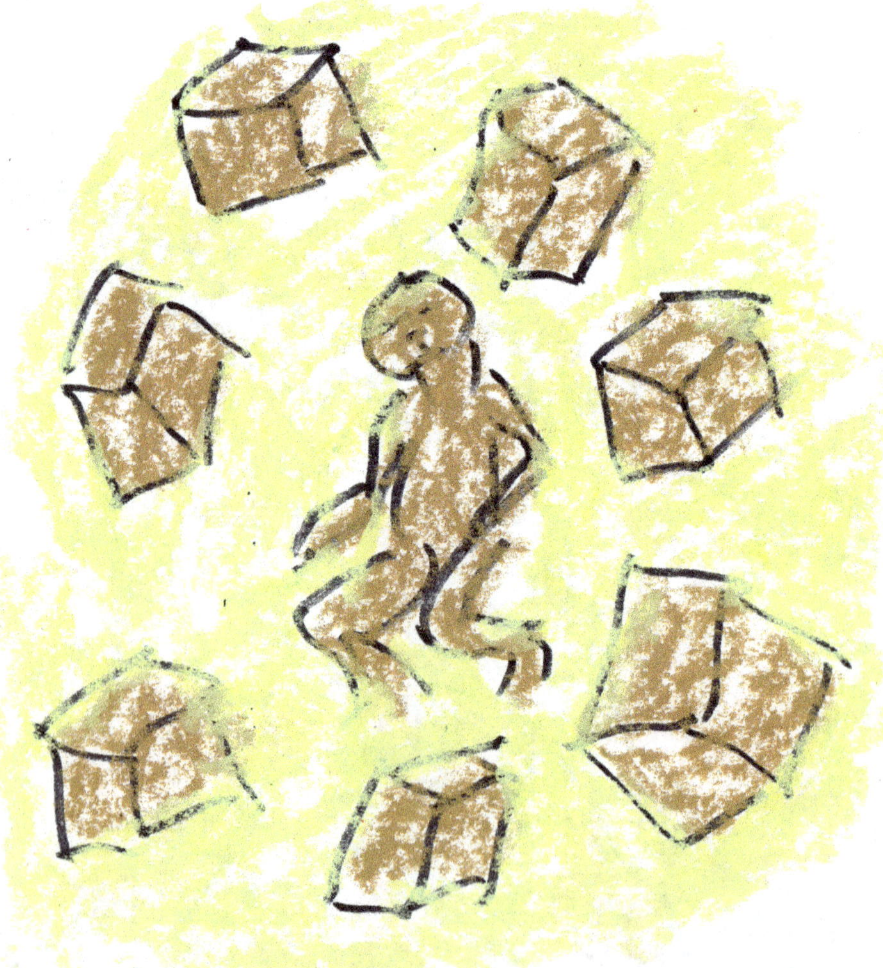

WERE IT NOT

FOR OUR INHERENT OBSESSION WITH VIOLENCE AS A MEANS OF PROBLEM-SOLVING

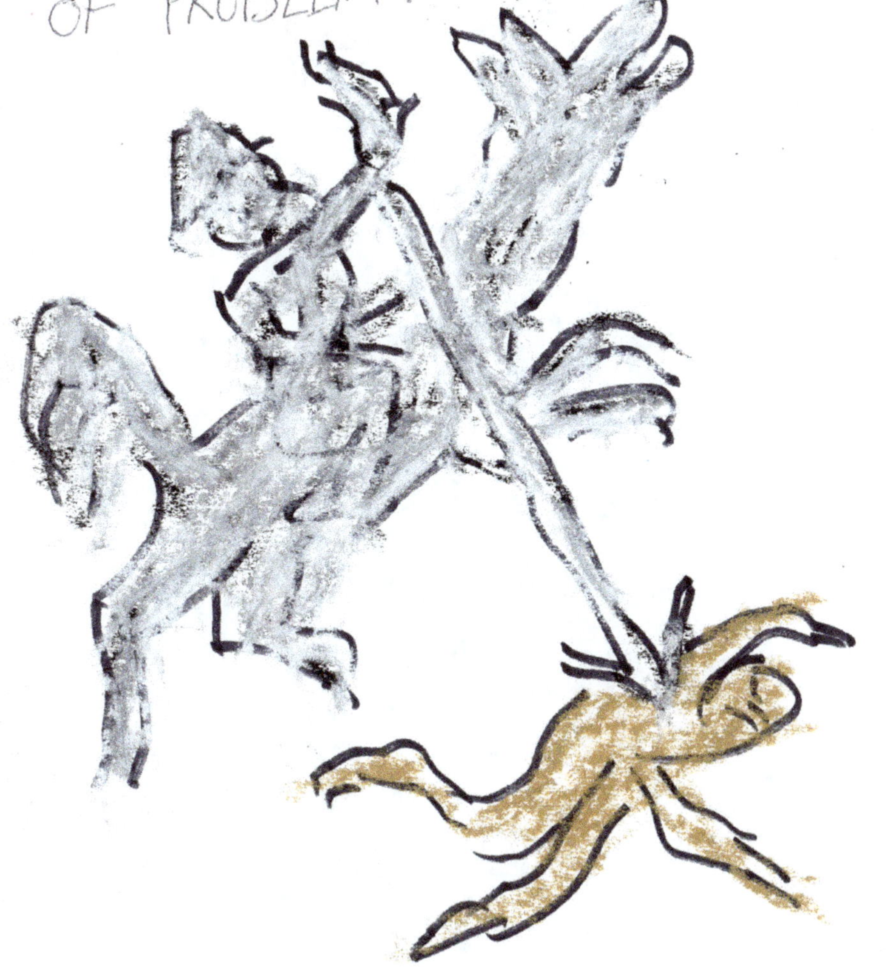

INSTEAD OF FOOD + ACCESS TO FOOD, INSTEAD OF HOUSING + ACCESS TO HOUSING, INSTEAD OF ACCESS TO NECESSITY + LIVELYHOOD. WE RESORT TO OUR SPECIALTY. OUR CURSE+ARROGANCE, OUR EXCEPTIONALISM, OUR US VERSUS THE ILL-DEFINED OTHER

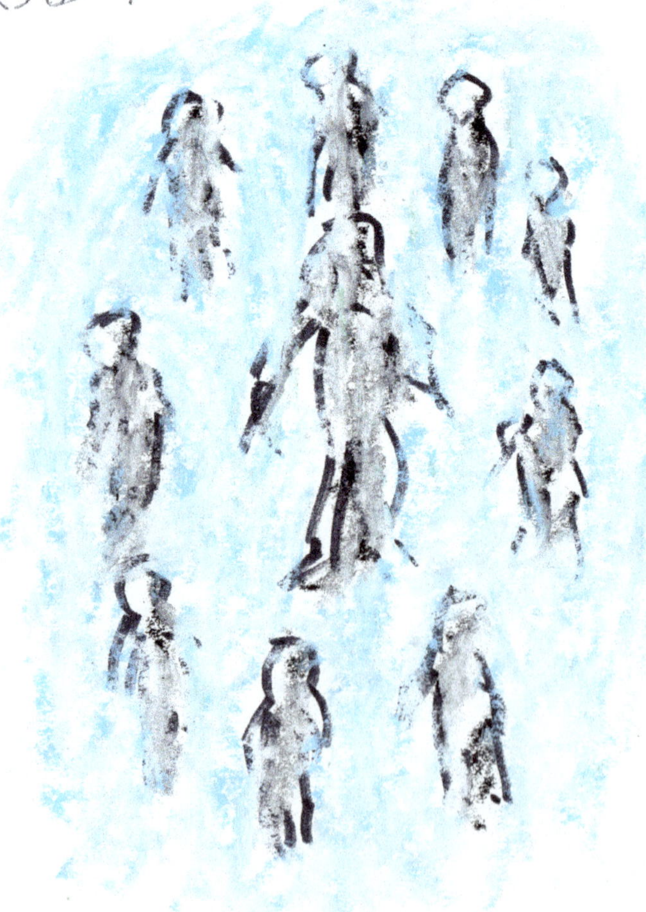

AND AS OUR

ARSENAL OF STRICTLY DEFENSIVE
WEAPONS AGAINST THE OTHER GROWS
+GROWS TILL IT OVERFLOWS INTO
SUFFERING REALITY

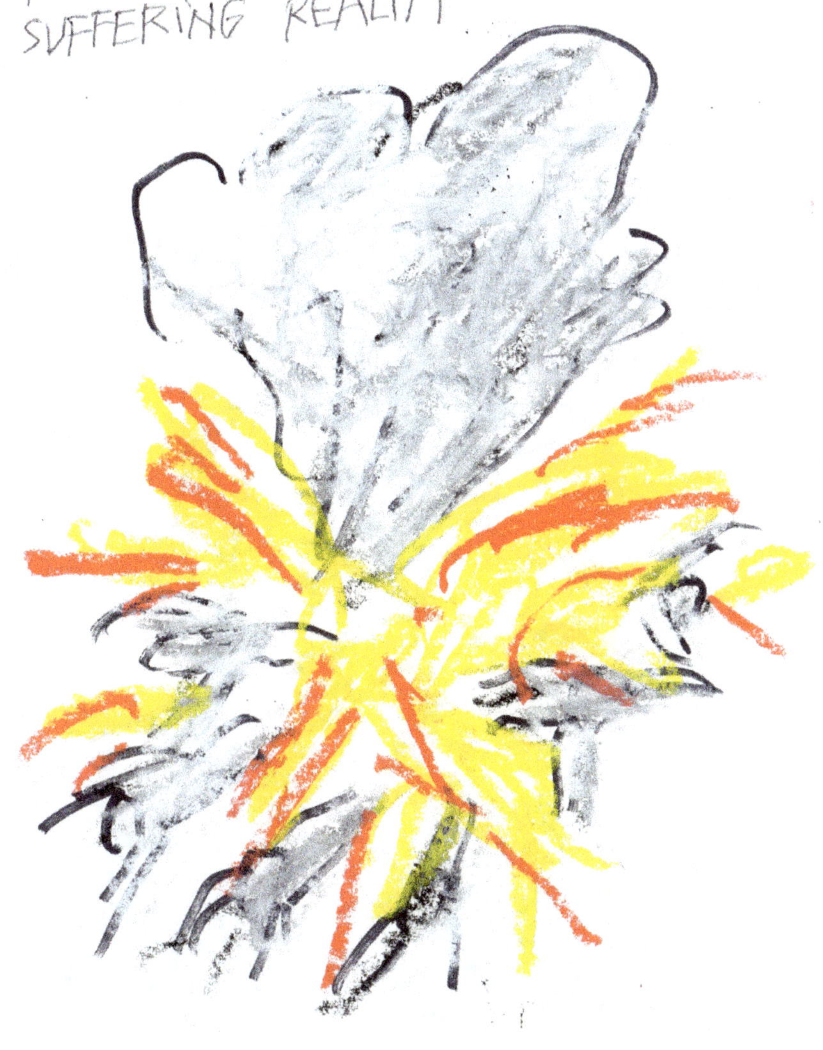

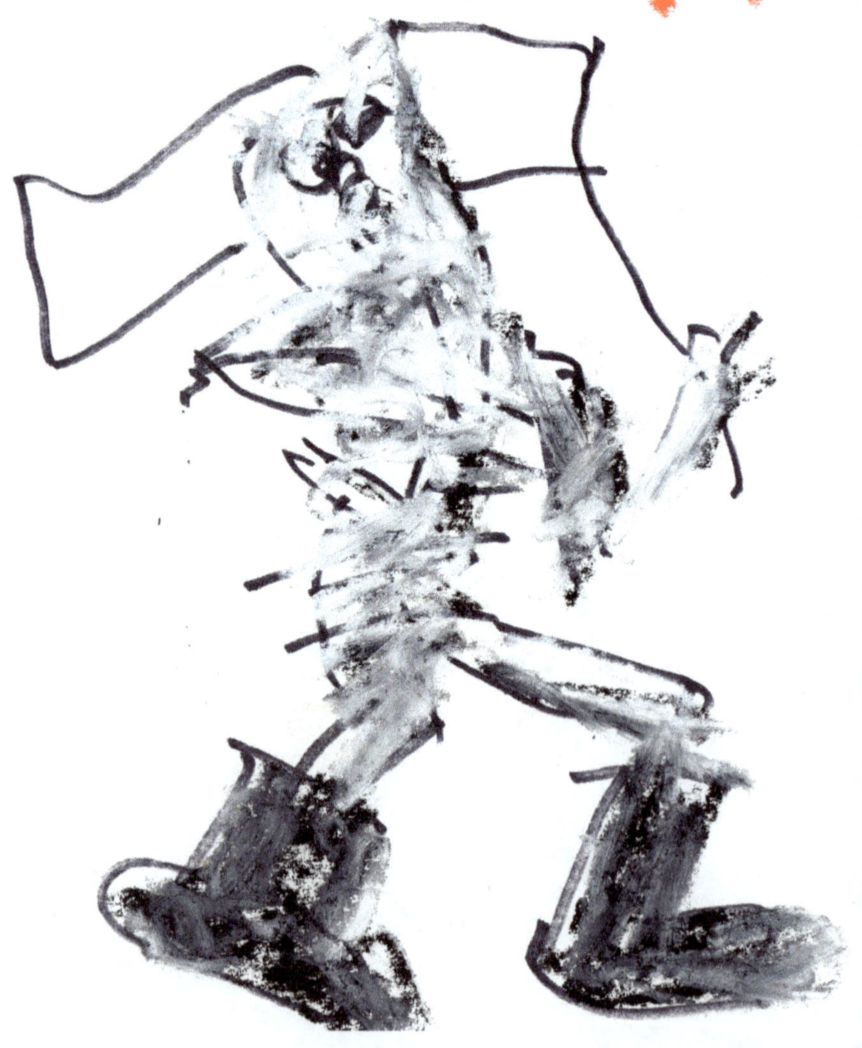
t WE YIELD TO
OUR HISTORY
WHICH iS WAR

THE POWER

OF OUR MOMS + GRANDMAS +
BABIES +TODDLERS HAS NOT
REACHED OUR HEART. YET

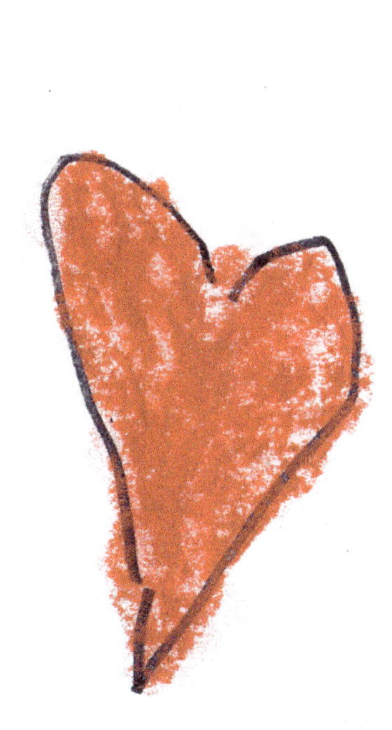

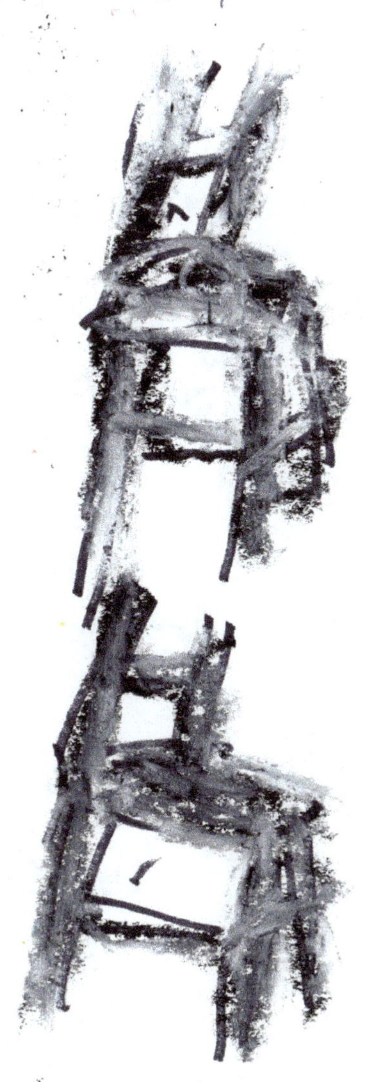

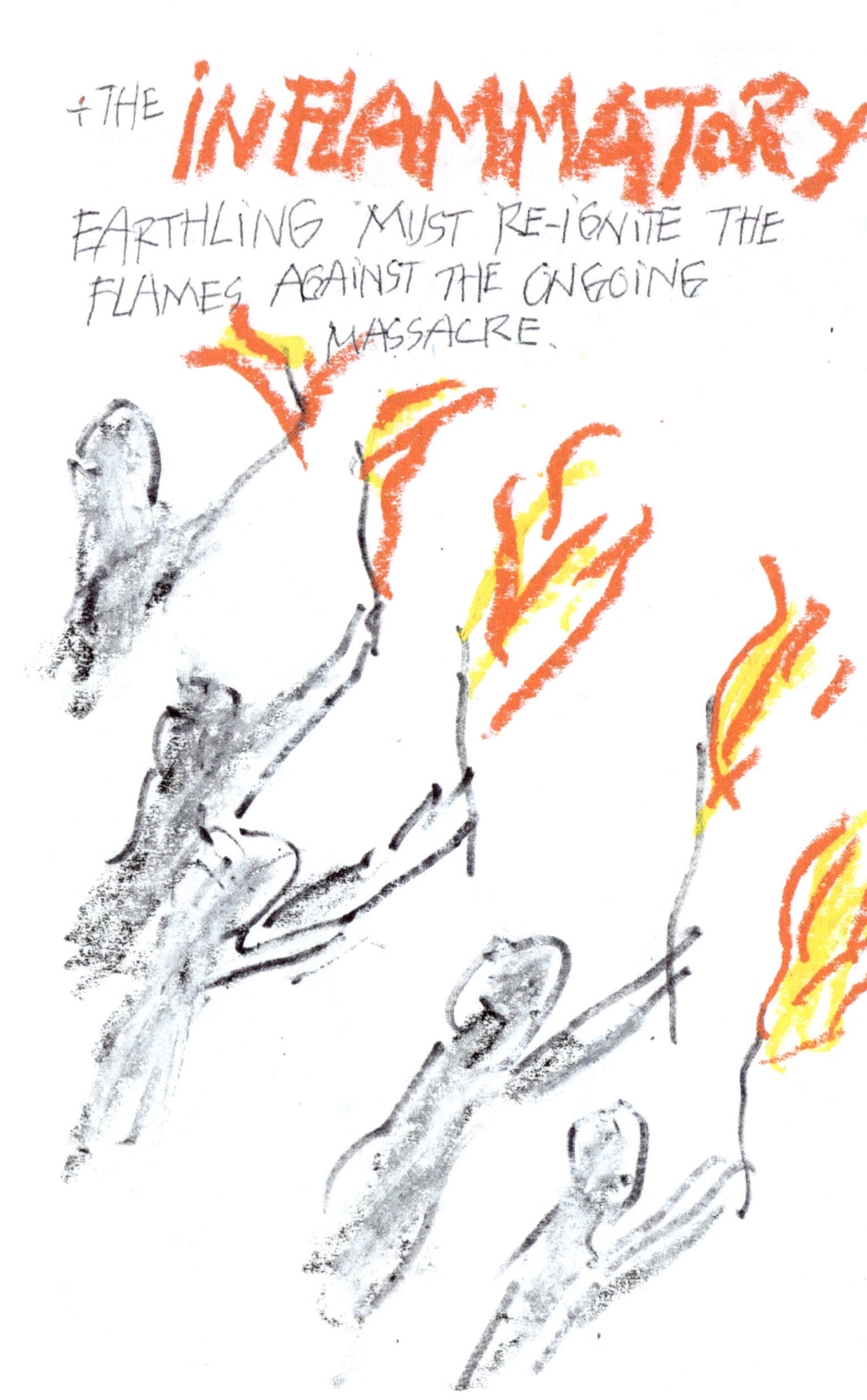
+THE INFLAMMATORY
EARTHLING MUST RE-IGNITE THE
FLAMES AGAINST THE ONGOING
MASSACRE.

POSSIBILITARIAN

WHAT

THE ACUMULATED EVIL OF THE WHOLE

①

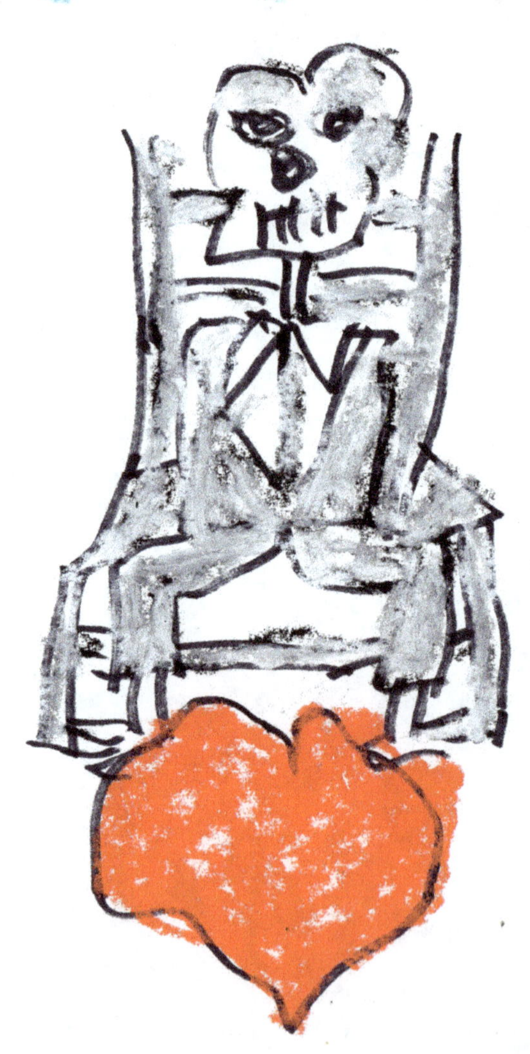

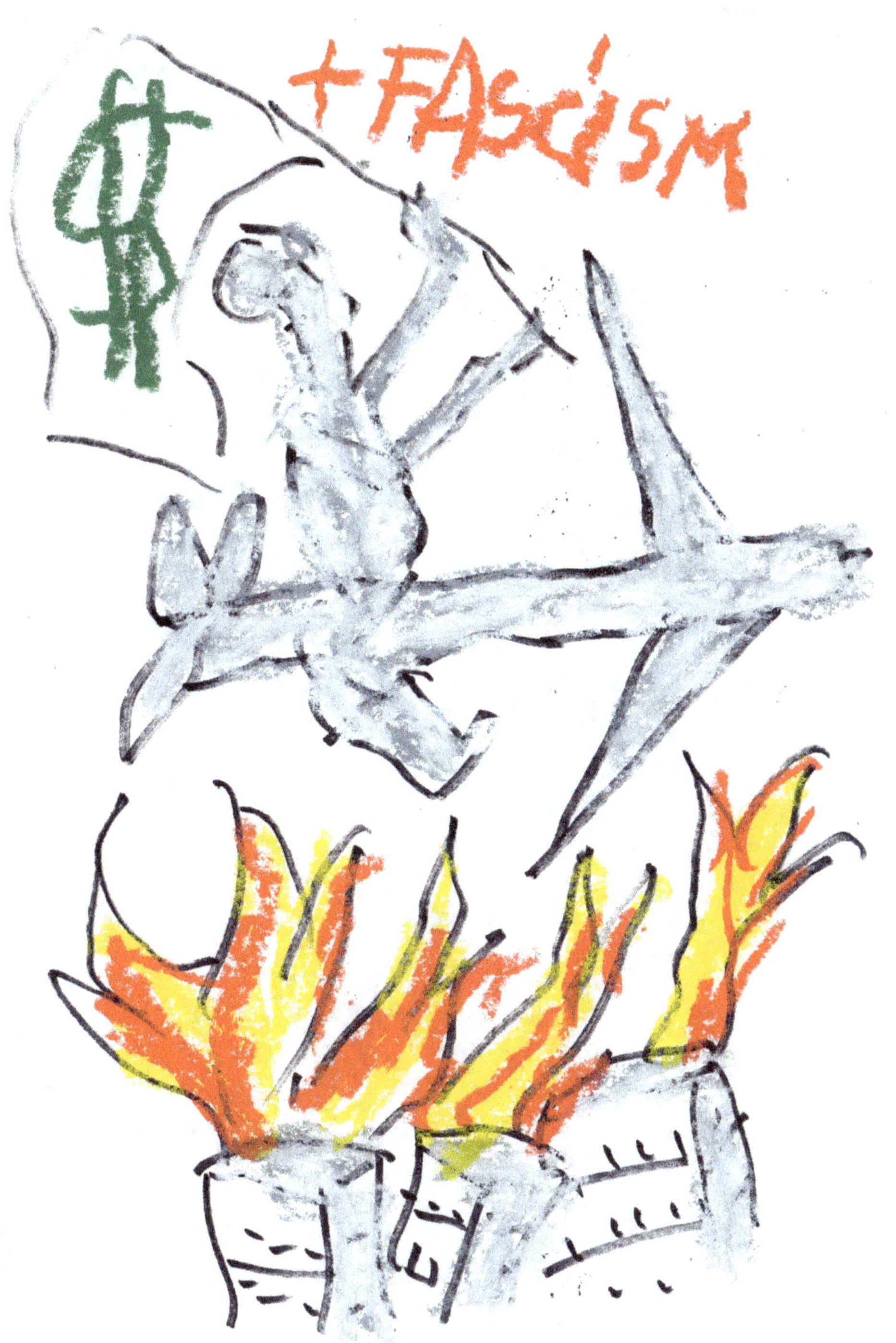

$
+ FASCISM

HAVE PRODUCED

THOUSANDS OF DEAD KIDS UNDER
THE RUBBLE OF GAZA

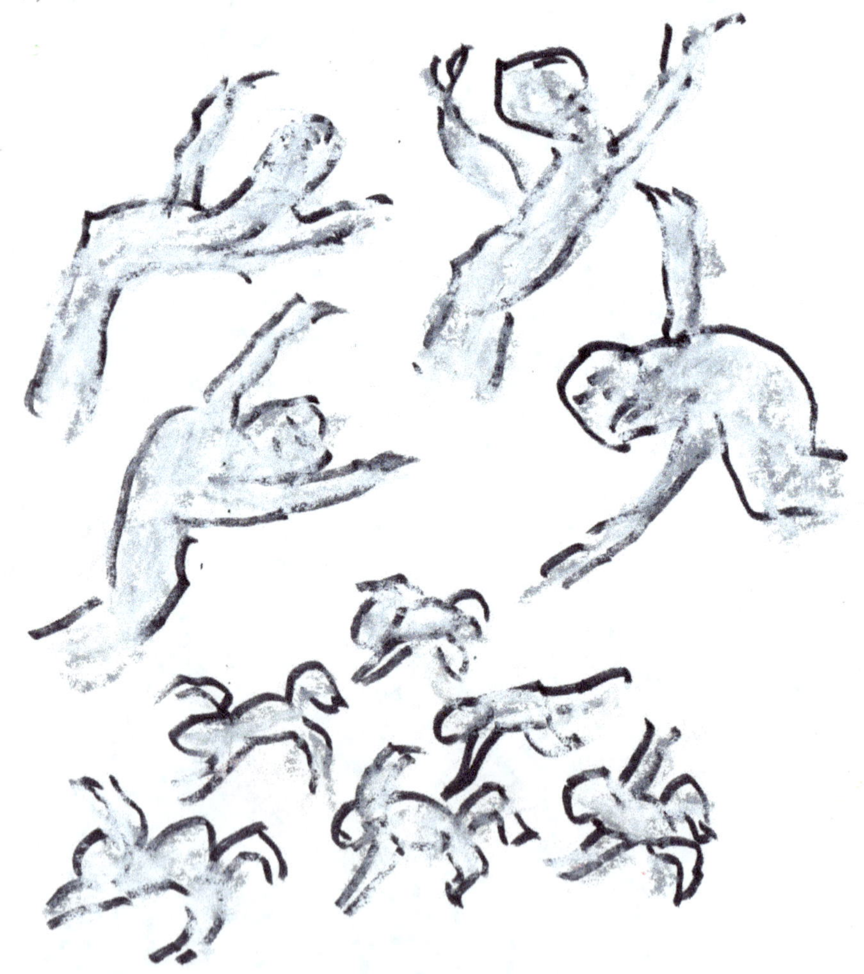

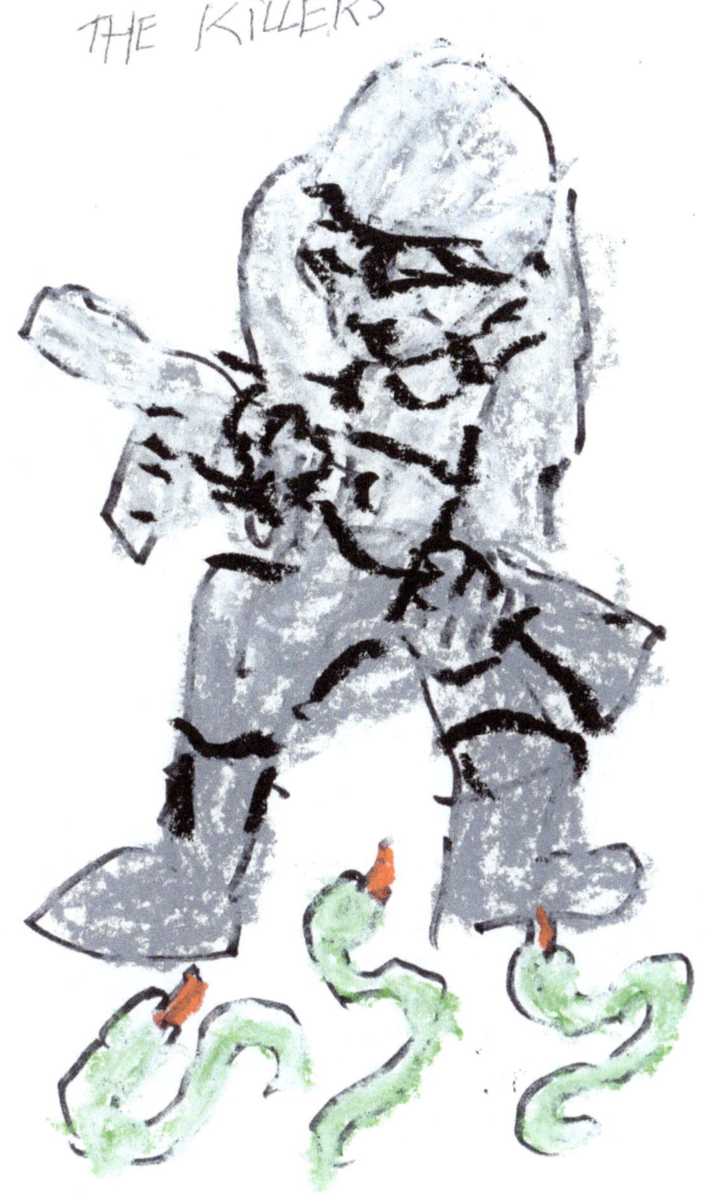

REFERED TO AS SNAKES, BECAUSE DANGEROUS TO THE KILLERS

+ INDEED THEIR

OBLITERATED FUTURE WILL FOREVER HAUNT THE EXECUTIONERS

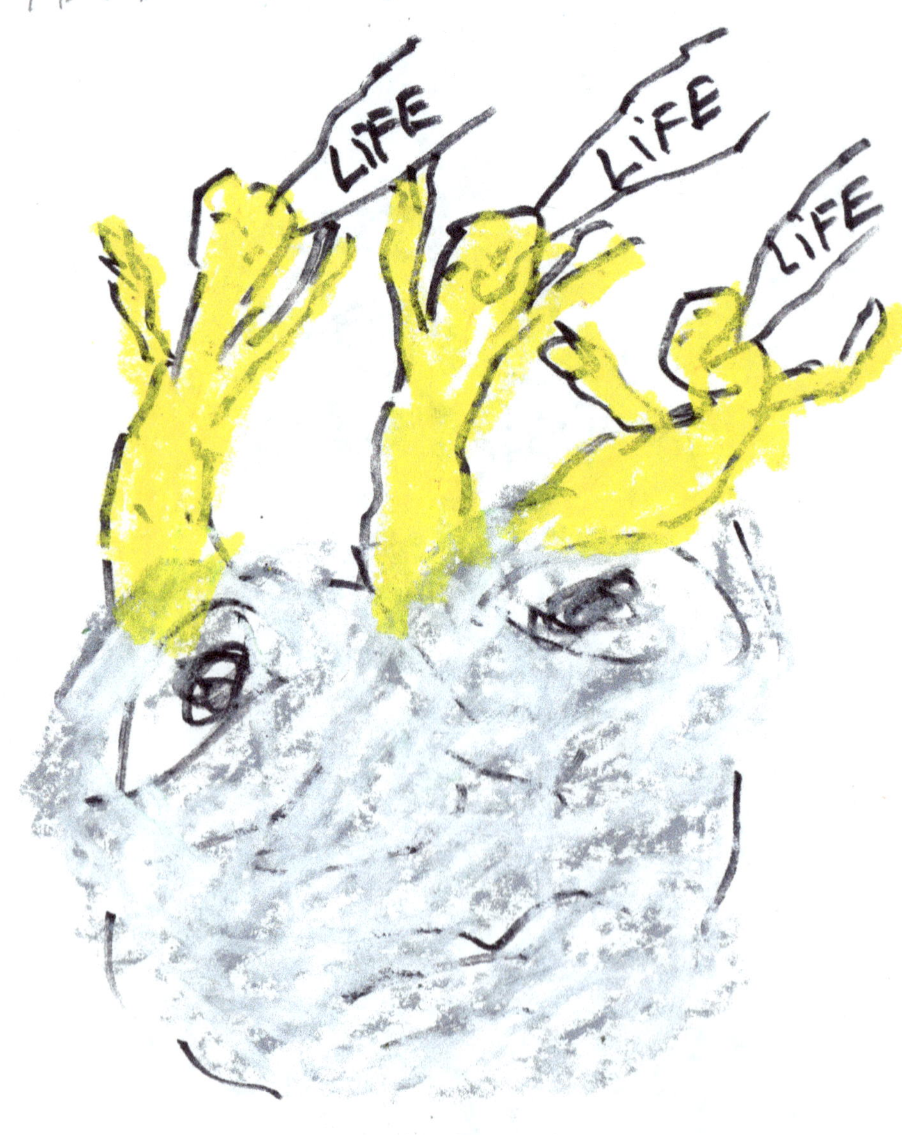

+ VOID ANY
PREDICTABLE FUTURE

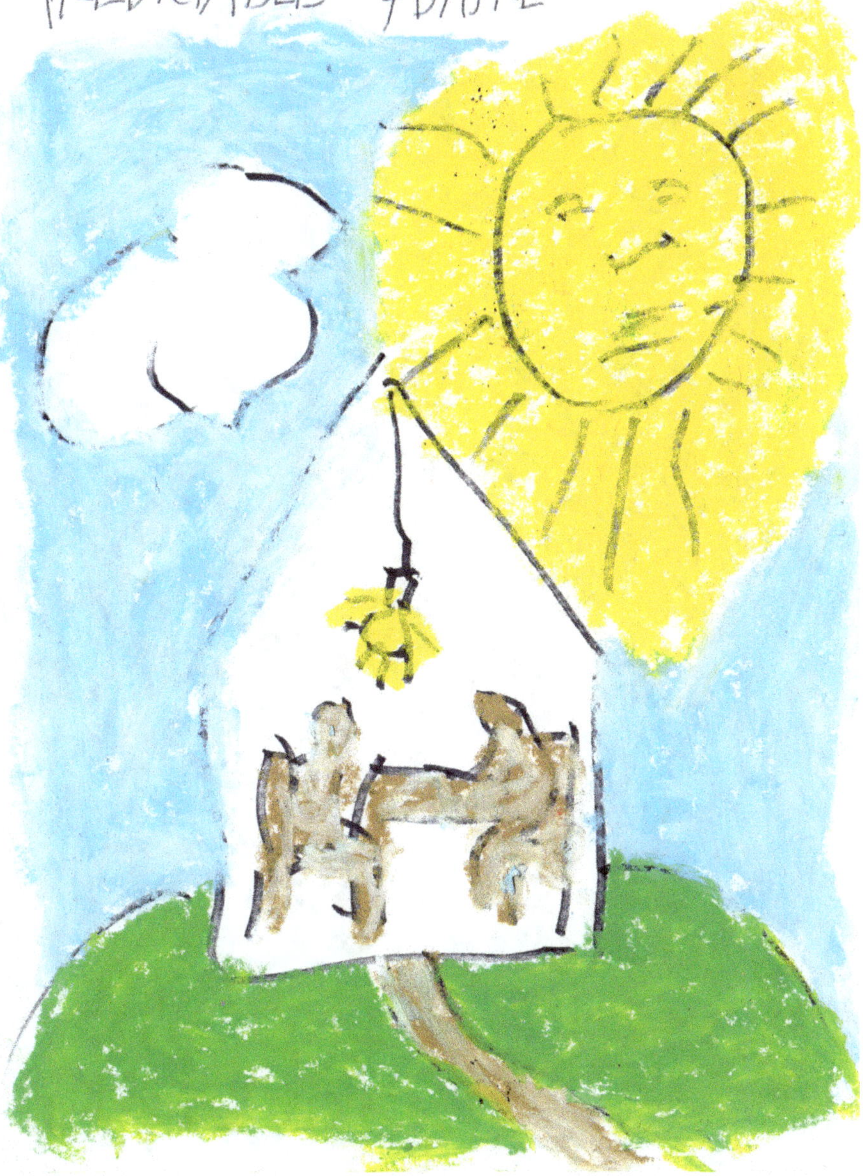

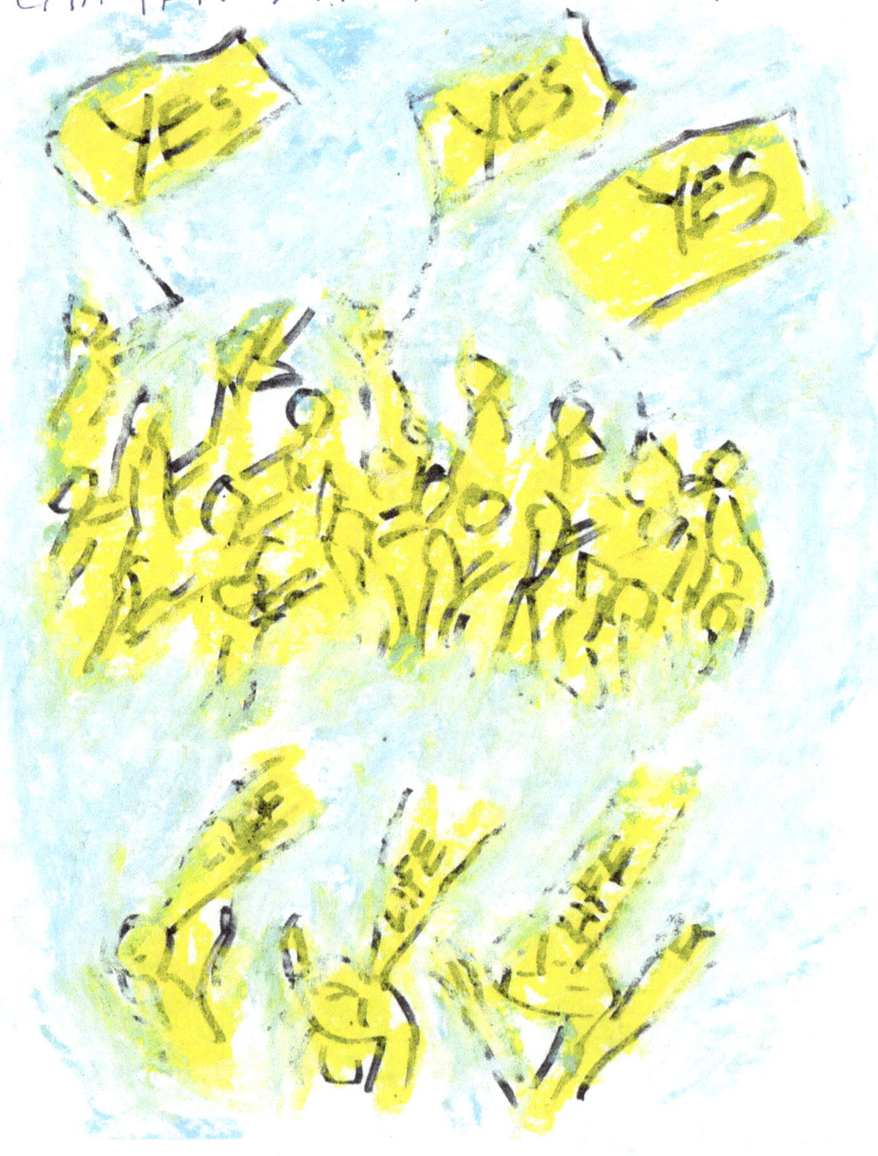
UNLESS A NEW
TONALITY LEARNED FROM THE
SCREAMING KIDS UNDER THE RUBBLE
CAN PERSUADE TO A NEW LIFE
YES
YES
YES
LIFE
LIFE
LIFE
LIFE

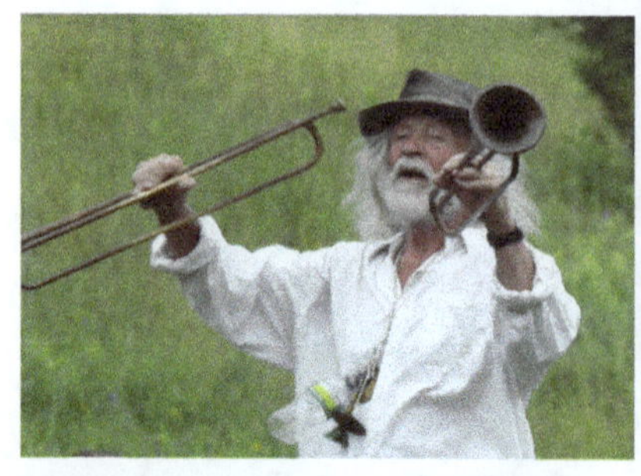

PETER SCHUMANN is the founder and director of the Bread & Puppet Theater. Born in Silesia, he was a sculptor and dancer in Germany before moving to the United States in 1961.

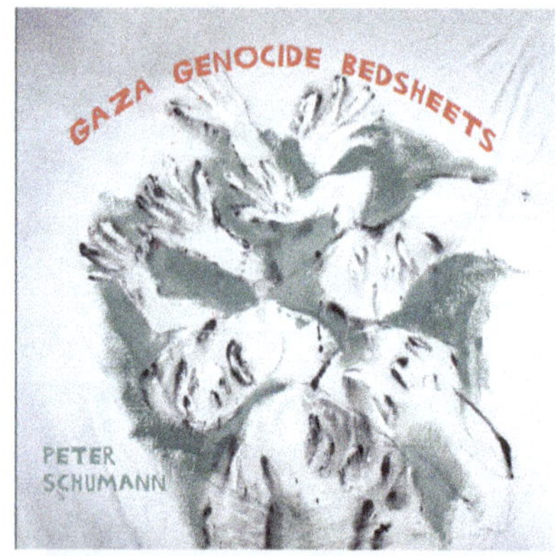

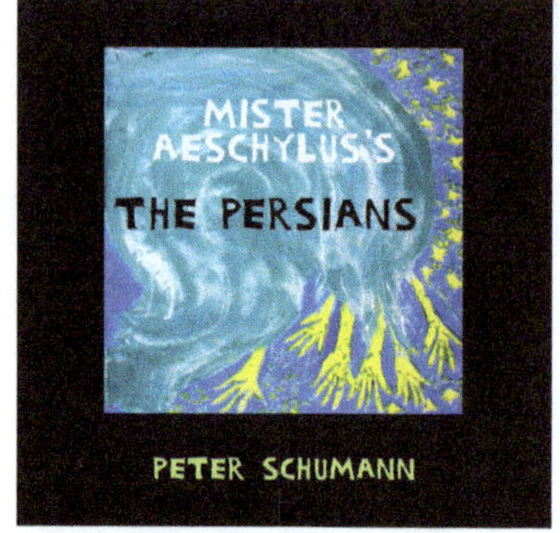

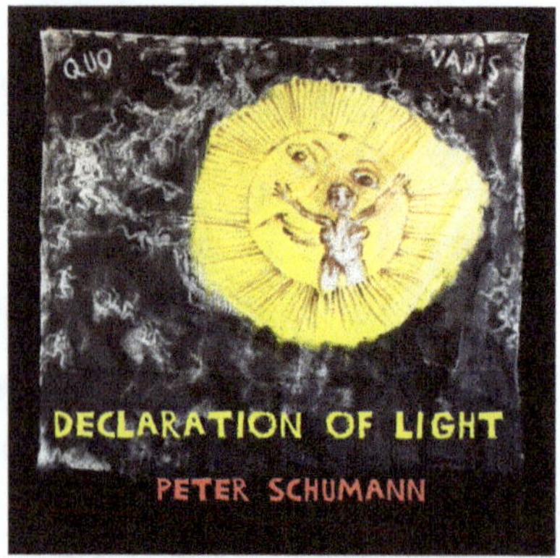

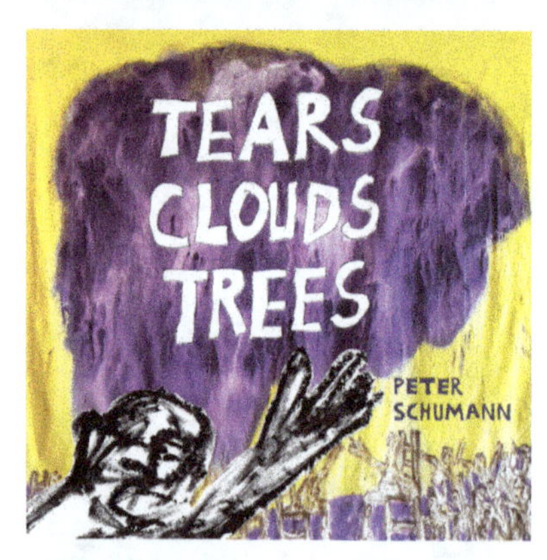

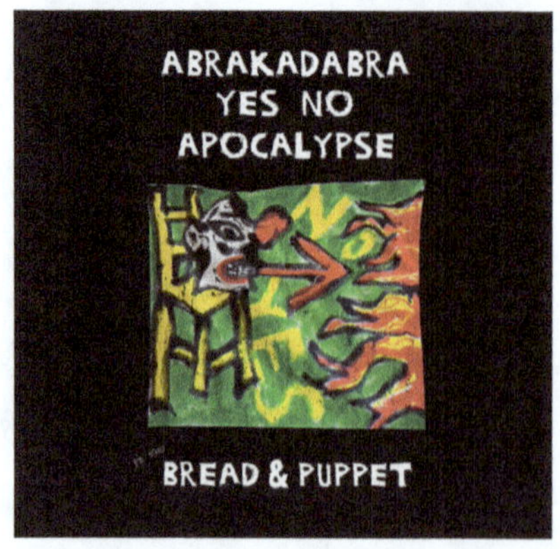

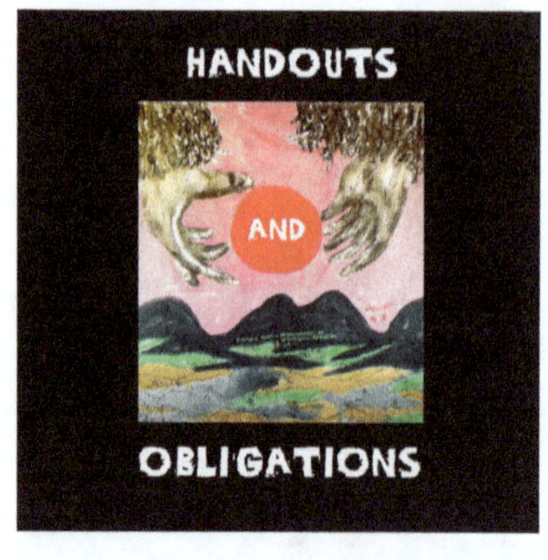

OTHER PETER SCHUMANN BOOKS FROM FOMITE

Diagonal Man One and Two
Planet Kasper One and Two
Faust Three
Es ist vollbracht/Mission Accomplished
Erbarme Dich/Have Mercy

Order books from
https://breadandpuppetpress.org/collections/fomite-press

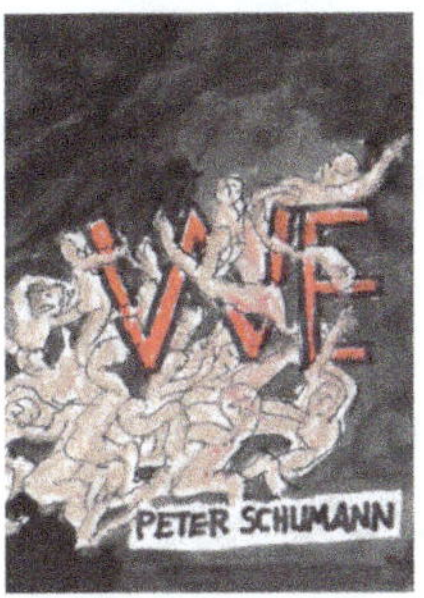

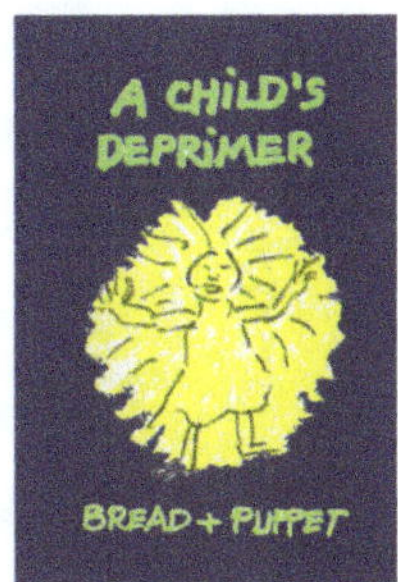

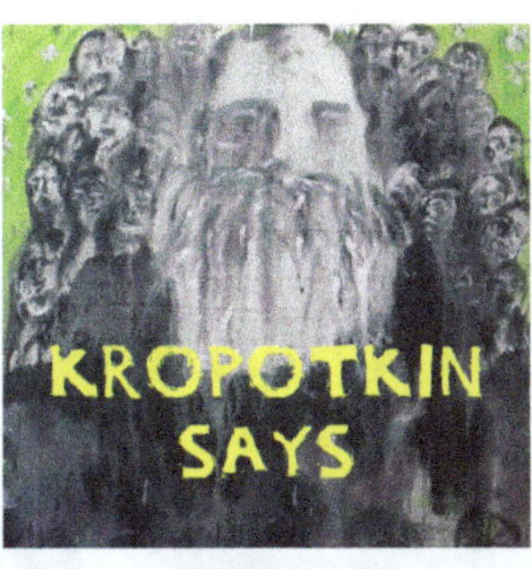

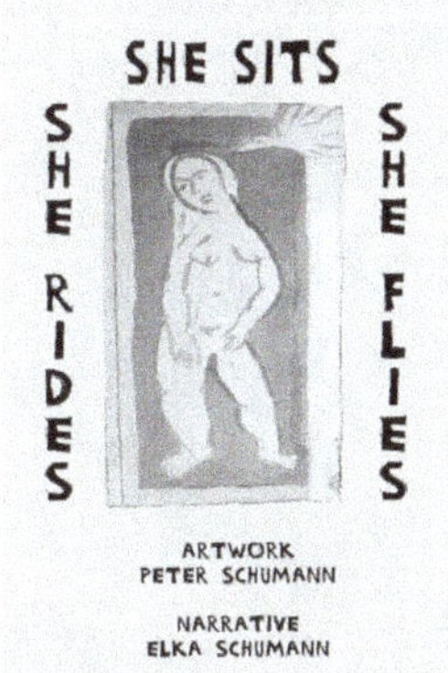

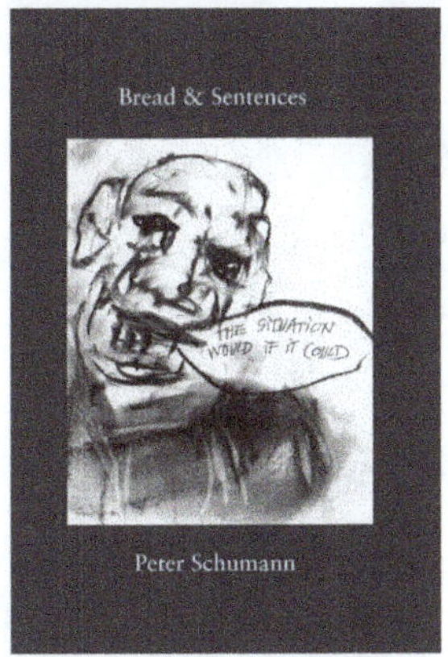

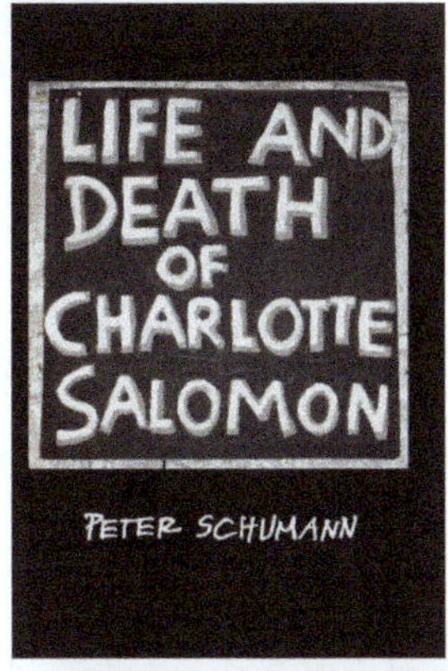

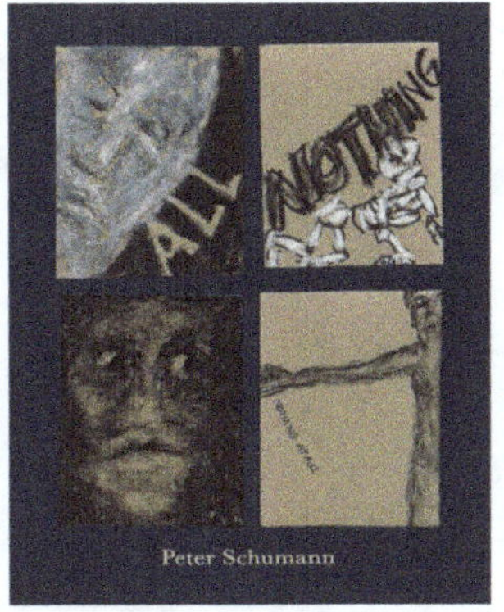

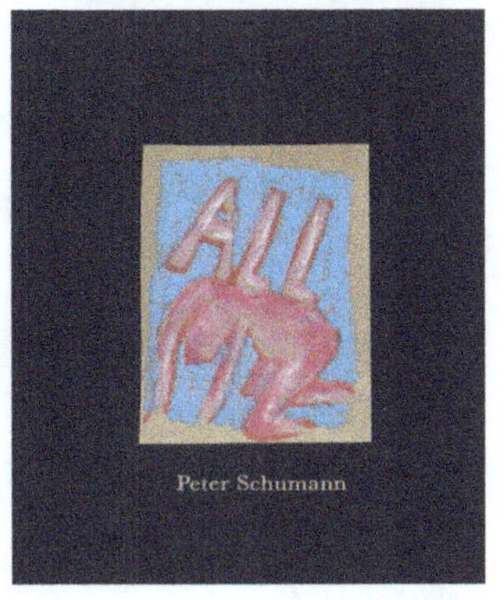

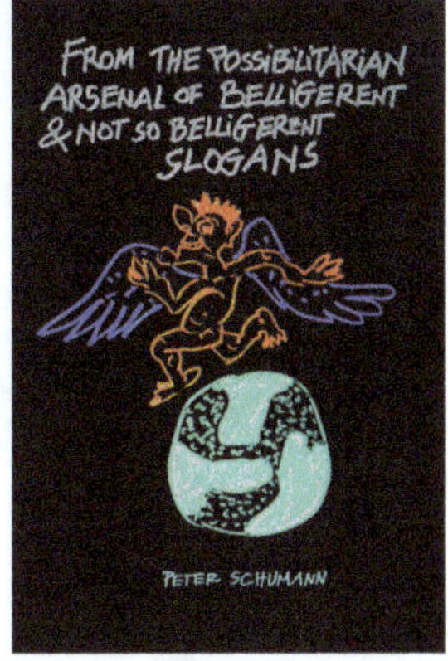